Editor Robert Stapleton
Managing Editor Jeff Marvel
Associate Editor Katie Peterson
Fiction Editor Jon Mann, Lenae Marsh
Poetry Editor Sophie Salerno-Dewald
Nonfiction Editor LuAnne McNulty
Web Manager Demetra Koras
Social Media Jennifer Delgadillo

Readers Bek Primrose, Brandon Butcher, Elizabeth Reames, Hannah Salsbery, Heidi Klein, Jennifer Delgadillo, Jennifer Schuster, John Strauss, Katie Shimer, Kaylee Gaddie, Lindsey Henderson, Monica Lewis, Paige Wyatt, Steven Ullberg, Sam Ferrante

Design & Layout Kayla E. / Design Altar

Copyright 2024 by *Booth* and contributors. All rights revert to artists and authors.

We publish new material on our website on the first Friday of every month, along with two print issues per year. We invite electronic submissions only from September 1 to November 30 and again from January 1 to March 31 at booth.submittable.com/submit. Full guidelines on website.

We are grateful for the ongoing support of the Butler University MFA program and the College of Liberal Arts & Sciences at Butler University.

ISSN 23332-4813
ISBN 978-0-9961641-3-9

A 1-year print subscription is $15. Send to:
Booth/Butler University
4600 Sunset Ave
Indianapolis, IN 46228

Visit us online:
booth.butler.edu

contents

Fiction

01   Auntie
Justin Noga

34   The Sinkhole
Adrián Pérez

76   The Delivery Boy
Rachel Salguero Kowalsky

101   The Girl Goes Missing
Courtney Craggett

116   Nude
Sam Fouts

125   Afternoon at the Wig Shop
Claire Stanford

136   The Rage Room
Mialise Carney

152   Frog
Tim Raymond

166   While We Can
Dan Reiter

Interviews

9   A Conversation with Viet Thanh Nguyen
Jennifer Delgadillo

105   A Conversation with Jo Ann Beard
Susan Lerner

Nonfiction

56   Asopao
Jerilynn Aquino

149   Girlhood Pentaptych
K.S. Dyal

Comics

64   Wolf
Jesse Lee Kercheval

Poetry

31   After Passing the Standardized Field Sobriety Test, I
Hannah Cohen

32   The First Time I Thought My Father Could Kill Me
Mimi Yang

33   In the Beginning, Forest
Hannah Marshall

59   Unusable Tarot Reading from the Passenger Seat of a Crashed Peugeot 205 (1997)
Fee Griffin

60   Resurrecting
Maggie Yang

62   After a Burial
Michael Beard

63   Augustine
Calgary Martin

131   Eumorpha Achemon; My Exoskeletal Self-Defense
Willow James Claire

132   (Heavy Metal) Boots
Naomi Leimsider

133   Mimaw Burning Sage
Erin Pinkham

134   epigenetics or: hope for easeful adaption
nicole v basta

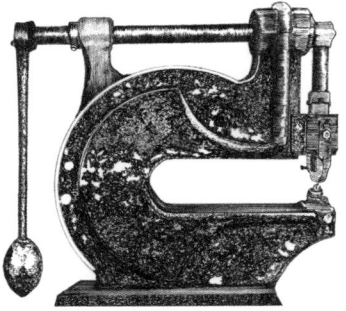

Auntie

JUSTIN NOGA

—

fiction

MY SISTER CRAB HAD FOUR KIDS THEN SIX THEN eight, and from her kitchen window we watched her new husband bandy about her new pool at her new house popping his hard-veined pecs in front of my pale pigeon of a husband. My husband, he cleaned toast crumbs from our soft bed. He never urged a child into me.

Are they getting along? I asked my sister. I can never tell.

How about we hear your side of this instead, Frog, and she dropped a bank statement onto the oak table. It said I had inheritance money, a confounding heap.

I said, We got money from Dad?

She thrust a sharp fingernail at the page. Is this not your address?

It is, but it must not be real because that's not *me* me.

Is this not your name, Frog?

No, I mean—

No?

I mean, I never signed this. I looked harder. Wait. That looks like your handwriting—the x's in place of dots? And this isn't inheritance. This is a loan. Are you taking loans out in my name?

How could you say that. She snatched the sheet away. How could you accuse me of a theft of Father's final leavings you yourself have conducted?

Where did you even get this?

That is piss talk. You're always trying to piss on me.

Is this why I'm getting collection calls all the time, Crab?

All the pain you've brought to me in life, to Father—I am done with you. Mother Mary in Heaven, help me get this woman out of my house!

In the pool, her husband and eight children were piled on my poor husband, who never realized it wasn't a joke. He floated up, belly down. Their white shih tzu, Chips, sat atop his drowned back, yowling in damp sorrow.

* * *

The man was deep in his 50s, and at the café when his face creased from the high noon sun, he appeared trapped in his 80s. An old face pocked and crumpled and dried on a stove.

Your sister says your husband is dead?

That is true.

She says you owe her money?

She says a lot of things.

It's not your first rodeo, I can tell.

Say again?

Blind date. First blind date. My head swims sometimes. Does that happen to you, Flipper?

My name's Frog.

What kind of name is that?

It's a family name.

Never trust family, he said. A bus rolled up across the street. Well, lovely parley this was, and he took a sip of wine and lit a cigarette and flicked it burning into a brittlebush and left the café and paid his fare for the bus with a pocket of nickels and quickly strode back out the bus and pointed at shop name after shop name until the café was found again and sat back down with me across his doublewide garden chair and said, blinking anew, Hello. I hear your husband is dead?

It's—not my first rodeo?

He smiled at that, the bush smoking behind him. Exactly what I was thinking.

* * *

My sister had 12 kids and two in the chamber. Her body was a taut bubble and mine still flat flab.

Can you even have kids at your age, Frog? she asked.

If I drink enough, maybe?

Crab pulled my hand to her belly as she lay on her long leather couch elbowed into the corners of her living room. Imagine, she said, imagine what the future will yield for my babies in this great nation: how many grown from me, how many grown from them, generations looking back and thinking, My great great gram was responsible for so much genetic kindness and love and we will never forget her throughout all time. Like what Father did for us. But better, you know? And me, not him, or you.

Unless there's a fire or something, I said.

What's that supposed to mean?

Like, and I pointed to a wildfire sprouted from the café across town.

Like that. Like when that gets here. Eventually it will. That's a lot of suffering you'll be on the hook for, the world you'd be bringing them into.

What a thing to say, Crab said. Two of her kids raced to hoist her up. Did you hear her, Francy? Francy was her newest husband. His shoulders were marbled in freckles, always peeling from sunburn.

What did that bitch say now? Francy yelled from the kitchen.

She says we're all going to die in a wildfire.

She didn't!

She did!

That bitch!

I know!

Outside my new husband idled in his swollen truck. He was staring into the sun, his eyes creased. He blinked anew. Watching me buckle in, he whispered, Did we already go inside?

**

My new husband's fat had winnowed off his body, and his brain had devoured itself and he sat with me on his hospital deathbed and told me now was the time to have kids.

Think about it, he said. Longevity past expiration. Pushing new life into this wide world and letting you and me be a part of that endless string of nature.

That's a long, lonely life you're pinning on me.

Kids bring joy when you're alone.

You mean you want me to be alone?

I mean what I say. Did I say it right, though?

I sleeved sweat off his cheeks. Kids cost a hefty buck, hon. You're not leaving me with much. The rental, the car lease. My first husband did the same, too, the poor man. Remember me telling you? Look where that's led me.

Am I not enough? What about the cans I've been saving? The lentils. The baby corn.

Gone.

Dang. He chewed on that. Did you ever meet my wife? She has money.

I am your wife.

The other one. We have kids. He leaned on his side with a moan, scooped from his pocket a wallet album of photos: photos of my sister and her 20 kids. Two up front are mine, Flipper. Or maybe those two?

That's my sister.

Who?

The woman. You've met her.

Is it? He looked worried. Ah. That's where she went.

* * *

Open casket was pricier, cosmetically intensive, but curiosity got the better of me once my sister said she'd pay for my second husband's funeral. I gave the funeral director a photo of my first husband from his 20s.

The man kept turning the Polaroid, holding it next to the coroner's headshot of my second husband. Your husband certainly aged so—what's the word?

Gracefully?

Let's just not define it, yes? He cupped a cold hand over mine. But we'll do our best, Mrs. Flipper.

* * *

At the wake the coffin lid was propped up in a grand way, all cushioning trimmed of woven gold rope. Inside lay my second husband. His nose and ears they carved down, the rest pillowed with botox. He resembled a weather-beaten mannequin with a soldered-on face updated for a line of surfer wear, a smooth new man I could love in between the men I loved. But his lips: a sour look. Sucked in. Sewn too taut.

I asked the funeral director, Is there a way you could puff his lips a bit before everybody comes? They were puffed more. More, I don't know, kissable?

Do—do you want people to kiss him? Is that what you're asking?

No, but, like, they should want to, yeah. Does that make sense?

No.

Could you do it anyway?

He sighed, bent over the body, squeezed the lips until they pudged out, shining. A seam popped. Propane odor leaked out.

Pee-yew, I said.

That's not good, the funeral director said.

Is that normal?

I—have to grab something, he said, and sprinted out the door and across the parking lot in long gallops and swallowed his body into a hedge.

Crab arrived. She wore matching black with her new husband, Wort. Wildfire from outside ate at their pantlegs, which Wort beat back down with his jacket.

But it's a dry heat, Wort said, and behind him my sister groaned.

Where are the kids? I asked.

My sister said, They're tending the car, duh.

I looked out the window. All 25 kids were there, blowing and spitting on the flames creeping across the blacktop toward the minivan, stomping out what they could with their little sneakered feet.

Cuties, I said. Dad would be proud of you.

Wasn't his favorite for no reason, she said.

Must have good lungs? Those kids?

You'd think. She cut a look at Wort. You would think that, wouldn't you, Wort?

Wort threw his hands up. I need the pisser, he said, and exited behind a nearby red velvet curtain, which covered a wall. His heels peeked out. A flask audibly unscrewed.

Crab wiped away a tear. Sometimes I wonder, you know?

Wonder what?

You wouldn't understand. You don't care about anything outside of yourself. Minimum for my respect is four kids, maybe three. It's like I'm not even talking to another adult, honestly. Crab leaned into my husband's coffin then, abruptly reeled away. Who the hell is that?

My husband.

Is it?

Who else would it be?

What did you do to him? She scrunched her nose. He smells off, too. He never smelled like that when I was with him.

You never said you two were married.

She rolled her eyes. If you could call that a marriage.

He said you took out a loan in my name and disguised it as coming from Dad.

Father didn't give me shit. I made my family from nothing.

I still get calls about the loan.

Just calls? You're bothering me at your husband's funeral about *just calls*? Now is not the time. She said, We're in mourning. She said, I need the pisser. She disappeared behind Wort's curtain. Both their heels stuck out. I heard giggling, another flask unscrewing.

I said to my dead husband, What a rodeo, right?

The light from the wildfire colored the gas seeping from his mouth. It rainbowed it across the room, wisped out the window like a wanting wick. Out there, I watched my sister's kids: dumping sippy cups on the marching flames, sponging the windshield clean of endless smokestain, vacuuming the leather seats of detritus and ember, all taking sweet care of mommy dear's new white minivan so her life would remain up to snuff. Even their white shih tzu, Chips, seeing these as half-measures, ran into the fire to scare it all away, but quickly poofed into his own vacuumable ashball.

I waved to them. They waved back, precious black smudges of hard work across their brows.

I was such a proud auntie then.

I looked at this in-between face of my husbands, dead before me. Maybe we should have kids? I said, Is it too late to think that? I said, That's silly of me, right? Gas swam in my brain. Fire washed the windows of the funeral home, lapped at its doors. Their lips looked kissably puffed, juiced, impatient for my touch, and I blushed hot, and puckered toward them, our real lives soon to start.

A CONVERSATION WITH
Viet Thanh Nguyen
JENNIFER DELGADILLO

—

interview

Memory seeds tradition, *celebration, family, friendship, but also rancor and the alternate realities that lead to the suffering of others. Viet Thanh Nguyen grew up understanding that artists and writers have the power to inflict harm. Growing up in the United States in the 70s and 80s as a refugee of the American war in Vietnam, Nguyen saw first-hand the impact of books, television, and film on the imaginations of Americans and beyond. He learned that stories play a role in the way people remember and misremember. Through his writing, Nguyen navigates the competing memories surrounding the war and the following generations that continue* living in the enormous crater left in the collective memory.

Viet Thanh Nguyen is a Vietnamese American professor and novelist. He is the Aerol Arnold Chair of English and Professor of English, American Studies and Ethnicity and Comparative Literature at the University of Southern California. He is a Fellow of the American Academy of Arts and Sciences.

Nguyen's debut novel, The Sympathizer, won the 2016 Pulitzer Prize for Fiction, the Dayton Literary Peace Prize, the Center for Fiction First Novel Prize, and many other accolades. He was awarded a MacArthur Foundation Fellowship and a Guggenheim Fellowship in 2017. Nguyen is a prolific writer. His other books are The Refugees; Nothing Ever Dies: Vietnam and the Memory of War, which was a finalist for the National Book Award for Nonfiction and the National Book Critics Circle Award in Nonfiction; and Race and Resistance: Literature and Politics in Asian America. He is a regular contributor as an op-ed columnist for The New York Times, covering immigration, refugees, politics, culture, and Southeast Asia. With his then-six-year-old son, Ellison, he co-authored Chicken of the Sea, a children's book. His most recent book is The Committed, the sequel to The Sympathizer. Next year, in addition to reading his books and columns, audiences will also be able to watch Nguyen's story about a man of two minds on the screen with HBO adapting The Sympathizer into a TV series.

Jennifer Delgadillo (JD): When did you first start imagining *The Committed* as a sequel to *The Sympathizer*?

Viet Thanh Nguyen (VTN): When I finished *The Sympathizer*, I did not think there was going to be a sequel, and when I set up *The Sympathizer*, it was supposed to be a one-off novel. However, while thinking about the next project, I realized I was still interested in this character and there was more to say about his life and his story from a novelistic perspective. And it works in terms of genre as well because it's supposed to be a spy novel, right? In genre, it's perfectly fine to have sequels and series and all of that. I also thought that there was more I wanted to learn about who he is as someone who's deeply political but whose politics have been challenged in all kinds of different ways.

Therefore, it was necessary to have a sequel so I could see what happens to a revolutionary after he's lost his revolution. Another part of it: It's not just his politics, it's also about himself. His masculinity is really problematic in *The Sympathizer*, as I discovered in writing the story, so I wanted that to be challenged, as well, and that's what happens in *The Committed*: He goes to France and investigates the French side of his heritage and the whole history of French colonialism, which is absolutely fundamental to him. It is fundamental to me as well and, you know, engages these political questions about revolution that I have been obsessing over since I was an undergraduate reading people like Frantz Fanon, who appears in the novel. Therefore, it was a way for me—fictionally—to deal with a lot of my own political and personal issues, too.

JD: You've mentioned that this is going to be a trilogy. Is it okay to ask about where the character is heading next?

VTN: *The Committed* is set almost completely in Paris, and he survives at the end, as he does in *The Sympathizer*. In the third and final novel—I think, because I haven't written it yet, but I love notes—his journey will begin in Central America because the CIA appears at the end of *The Committed*. The CIA will continue to play a role in the final novel, and the reason why I think he's spirited away to Central America is because the point in time here is 1985 and a lot of the things that the United States and the CIA were doing there in the 1980s were a direct continuation of what they were doing in Vietnam and Southeast Asia in the 1960s and 1970s.

To me, these are not discrete events. These are all part of the American global view of the United States' place in the world as well as the role of communism and the need to suppress any idea or hint of communism, wherever it appears. It appeared in Central America, and the United States did some very terrible things there. The final novel, then, to me, is an American novel in the sense of the greater America, not just the United States.

So it begins in Central America, but we will come back to North America because a lot of other interesting stuff was happening in the 1980s, which is my decade in terms of my adolescence and identification. Also, I want to work out things about the politics in the 1980s in the United States that were influential to me, things like

Ronald Reagan, redressing reparations with Japanese Americans, and the rise of women-of-color politics. All of that was taking place then and I think will appear in the final novel.

JD: You've spoken before about how anger played a key role in writing *The Sympathizer* and *The Committed*. Do you have advice for writers who feel anger, but are not yet able to put their feelings on the page?

VTN: Oh, I think that anger is a very tricky emotion. For me, it was important when I was in college, because it gave me the ability to articulate a lot of things that weren't articulated for me in adolescence, and anger really gave me both focus and a lot of passion. However, throughout my life, the anger has ebbed and flowed, which I think is a healthy thing because to be angry at the same pitch I was angry at when I was 19 would be hard to maintain for decades and decades.

Dealing with anger has been a matter of trying to figure out when it's appropriate. I think anger, like every other emotion, can be excessive, so it's not just anger that is the problem. Too much love is a problem. Too much hate is a problem, right? Being able to modulate the anger was really important in being able to recognize when I wasn't angry enough—that was *very* important. I feel as though in my 20s and 30s, I wasn't angry enough. I was focused on becoming a professor and dealing with academia, so I kept down the anger, which was perhaps necessary to survive. However, in retrospect, it was also not great for me as a writer.

In my 30s and 40s, it was about trying to get the anger back and trying to reach the sort of moment of idealism I experienced in my late teens and early 20s when the anger was also very important. I think that the events of the Trump era in my life also taught me that anger can be excessive in very problematic ways. The anger of the extreme-rightwing has been terrible for the country, but it's also provoked anger in me that was in many ways excessive, as well. So, those binary politics of action/reaction that characterized, I think, the Trump era but also characterized things like moments of warfare that have shaped my life could be problematic.

In a sense, I've had to also take a step back in the last couple of years in regard to my anger because it's felt better to not be angry all the time and be provoked by other people's anger. So, my only advice in this area is: Don't be afraid of your anger. At the same time, don't be overwhelmed by it, and learn how to use your own emotions and not have your emotions use you. That's the hard part, I think. There are a lot of people who also tamp down their emotions, which is also not good. It's very tricky to figure out how to be able to recognize the usefulness of your emotions, recognize when you're being overwhelmed by your emotions and harness them for your own purposes. Of course, this is true for every emotion, not just anger.

JD: In both *The Sympathizer* and *The Committed* your main character reads a lot. Why is it important for you to drive his story through his love of literature?

VTN: Well, because I think that not everybody loves literature, but some people do, so why not talk about it in books or movies? God forbid. Also, it's partly autobiographical. I love literature. I love reading and wanted to give a prominent place to that in my books. I was also driven by the idea that ideas are powerful. Look at the history of the 20th century and all the revolutions and calamities and struggles, etc.: They were driven by ideas, whether by capitalist ideas or by communist ideas. These ideas could have been expressed in very knotty and complicated ways by Marx or Adam Smith or whatever, and the average person may not have been reading these things, but the ripple effect of those ideas was tremendous.

So it seems utterly reasonable that someone who is deeply curious about the world and is serious about political change would want to read books, would want to read ideas, and when you look at the history of revolutions and so on, it's not just the philosophers and the academics who were reading these dense books or changing things. Actually, it's often everyday people whose lives have been touched by political ideas. Sometimes, they end up going to prison, for example, and in those places, ideas circulate. A lot of revolutionary education happens in prisons, where people are reading books.

In *The Sympathizer* and in *The Committed*, the discussion is sometimes very learned—there are characters who are professors in these books— and then sometimes the discussion is not necessarily learned, but the books are there. So, that's why in *The Committed*, it was important for me to have the muscle in the brothel be a guy who was big and Black and read books. I don't see a contradiction in that. Some people might, but that's the point. It's not just the effete professor in his fancy apartment in Paris who is reading stuff. It's also these folks who are lying low. The muscle is taking his time, and he's someone who I think is capable of revolutionary change, and it's taking place in a brothel. Again, none of that is contradictory to me.

Look, I'm Catholic. So, I think about how in the Bible, there are stories of revolution that Jesus led and everything—it took place among the people who are not the elite. It took place among the people who would be considered the lowest of their social classes. And so, that's partly what's being represented in these novels.

JD: Your short-story collection, *The Refugees*, is atypical in that it manages more than just the assembling of a collection of stories. You're painting a nuanced portrait of refugees. What was the process of assembling that collection? How did you decide what stories should be part of it?

VTN: In writing that book, I learned how to become a writer. I taught myself, through trial and error, different fiction techniques, but I was also thinking about trying to write a book that was greater than the sum of its parts. Sometimes, I read short-story collections and some individual stories may be brilliant, but it seems to me that the collection is just a random assortment of pieces. Some of the books that have been the most influential for me, in terms of short stories, have been James Joyce's *Dubliners* or, more recently, Edward P. Jones's *Lost in the City*. It felt to me that these were books that were also about places and groups of people and that was very deliberate on the part of the writers.

As I was trying to be a writer, I thought, Well, I also want to write about Vietnamese people, and I want to say something about getting these experiences collectively, as well. So, that was an easy decision, to say that everything would be about or mostly about Vietnamese people. And if it's not about Vietnamese people directly, it's about people who interact with Vietnamese people, because obviously we don't just hang out with each other all the time. So, that was one way of setting the parameters of the book, and the other way was to make it thematically about refugees. Therefore, it's not about all Vietnamese people in Vietnam, it's about this particular refugee experience. It's cohesive in one way, but even when we're talking about a very specific subset of people, not everybody's the same. I was also thinking about Sherwood Anderson's *Winesburg, Ohio*. It's about people in a small town. They're all Americans. They're all Midwesterners, and so on. However, they're not all the same. Therefore, if we can think that about white people, obviously we can think that about any other population.

In writing the book, it was also very important for me to think that even if Vietnamese people are divided into refugees and diaspora, even within that subset, there's vast diversity. So, my job was to try to capture some of that diversity. I tried to make the stories about different people, even if they were all Vietnamese and refugees. In fact, I actually did use a spreadsheet to help me not just write about myself.

Even if these are Vietnamese people and I'm a Vietnamese person, the stories are not all about Vietnamese men in their 20s and 30s, and that was crucial because I have read collections about white male authors that are all about young white men. Okay, well, that is cohesive, but it's also going to be limiting. I felt that when it comes to these questions of self and otherness that are important for a lot of us who are writers of color, it's important to recognize that sometimes we're the "other" in relation to other people, but sometimes other people are "others" to us. That otherness can be a different race, but sometimes otherness can be your mother, otherness can be your family. Otherness can be people within your community, and that raises a challenge for me, as a writer, about how to write about that otherness. It's an ethical, ethnic, aesthetic, and political question. If we challenge white writers for their inability to deal with various kinds of otherness, then I need to challenge myself as well.

JD: I do have one more question about *The Refugees*, about the story "The Other Man," because it stood out to me from the other stories. The bonds of family, tradition, the past—those are present in most of the stories but not in "The Other Man." I read it as a story about the importance of giving yourself permission to cut ties with the past, with tradition, with family, when they don't serve the person that you need to become. Could you talk about why you thought it was important to make that point?

VTN: I grew up with complicated feelings about what home and community meant. On the one hand, I always felt welcomed at people's homes and certainly felt that I was home in my parents' home, but on the other hand, I often felt very uncomfortable for different reasons. The Vietnamese-refugee community itself is afflicted with all kinds of traumas, tensions, and so on. In my own parents' home, I felt like I didn't fit in. I wanted to be a different kind of person than what my parents wanted me to be. Looking at the larger Vietnamese-refugee community, I could also see a lot of in-fighting and backstabbing and divisiveness. And then I could look at other Vietnamese families and see a lot of intimacy and loyalty, but then a lot of terrible things could also be happening in these families: infidelity, alcoholism, abuse, that type of stuff. I could see that people were very conflicted by these relationships. They wanted to leave, but they never could.

I left at my very first opportunity, and that's probably a tribute to my parents. They didn't want to hang on to me so tightly that they couldn't let me go. However, I have seen enough Vietnamese families to know that some people never did leave when they should have. It would have been better for them, but for a number of complicated emotional reasons, they didn't. For me, family and home are things that are not sentimental. They can be nurturing, and they can be destructive, and both can happen at the same time.

I don't think this is unique to immigrants and refugees, but if you're an immigrant or refugee, family and community are supposed to be your bulwark against the larger society—another reason why it's hard to leave. And so, there's no right or wrong choice in these circumstances. Maybe if I'd stayed, I would have been a different person. Maybe that would have been a better situation. I have no idea. Clearly, people have left. People have transformed themselves by leaving, and that's the choice that this particular character is making, and we don't know what the consequences will be. That's why it's a short story, you know? I thought, Maybe I should have written a novel about this particular character and seen what the unfolding consequences of his actions are for himself and for his family, but a short story is about capturing the moment in time and leaving us on the precipice of a situation where something dramatic is happening. Something very important is happening. Something very life-changing *has* happened for this character, and that's enough for that moment. However, we know that it's life-changing to stay and it's life-changing to leave, and it's such a complicated decision for so many people. That's what makes it a great moment for a short story to focus on.

JD: In the essay "On Victims and Voices" in *Nothing Ever Dies*, you describe the importance of authenticity and how it never really eliminates ventriloquism. Do you have any advice for ethnic writers about ethically addressing this issue?

VTN: I think it pays for so-called ethnic writers to be very conversant about the entire situation—when we're talking about the United States—within the United States, where their literature functions. I don't think it's enough for an ethnic writer to say, "I just want to write my story," because I don't think that's a freedom that we have as ethnic or minority writers.

If you're a majority writer, you can say that—I don't think that's ethical, either, but you have all the power and the freedom that's granted to you because you're part of the majority, whether you're a man or a white man or just a white person. You have a lot of freedom and privilege granted to you by that because when you write, you write as a part of the majority, and the audience that receives you will be part of the same majority. There will be a lot of understanding, implicitly, that takes place, and it's all taken for granted.

However, when you're a so-called ethnic or minority writer, you're dealing with a much more complicated terrain within your own community that's imposing expectations of authenticity on you, but you're still within this so-called majority community that's imposing its own expectations of authenticity on you. It is certainly an aesthetic concern at that point, but it's an aesthetic concern that's inseparable from the politics and economics of the larger society in which your community is embedded— all the various inequities that are involved there, which saturate every relationship, including not just the act of storytelling but everything in the world of literature.

I call it an illiterate industry because it is, because there are economics involved, agents and publishers and reviewers, and all of that is in the industry. It's not just about the art—it's about all the other inequities and assumptions that I've mentioned. So, if you, as a so-called ethnic or minority writer, walk into this and say, "I just want to tell my story," and you're completely uninformed about this environment, and you're completely uninformed about the entire way by which your people have been read, and you're uninformed about how your people have already written and been received, you're setting yourself up for so many mistakes. Now, you could be the genius that, as a naive person, has so much talent you can blow up in this whole situation—that could happen. However, I think that for the overwhelming majority of writers in this situation, if they're uninformed, their literature is not going to be very good because they don't understand all the various assumptions that are imposed on them. They also will not have seen how literature functions as a genre. For instance, I can look at any single category of literature in this country, let's say Asian American literature—it's a genre. And if you read a hundred books of Asian American literature, you will see that there are tropes that emerge. Some of them are good and some of them are bad, but as with every trope, if it's been done by 99 other writers and then you do it yourself, that's not going to be very interesting.

Now, if you know that the trope exists and you decide to use it and subvert it, that's interesting. Also, the trope exists because of various kinds of historical and social pressures and so on from inside and outside the community, but you have to have read all of that in order to know that.

Therefore, I think, fairly or unfairly, the so-called ethnic or minority writer has a big challenge ahead of them. Not only do they have to learn the art, which is a universal art, they have to learn the particularities of their own history alongside literary and political history in order to see that the literature is inseparable from all of that—the tropes and the techniques, etc.

Given all that, the so-called ethnic or minority writer can then con-

front the questions of authenticity and voice in an ethical artistic and political fashion. However, if you're naive and you don't know these kinds of things, you're going to repeat the worst tropes of authenticity and voice and ventriloquism and all of that.

Even though the world of literature is supposed to prize originality, the literary industry, especially when it comes to so-called minorities, is built on cliches and assumptions and prejudices. It's very easy for the so-called ethnic or minority writer to fall into those, to reiterate those, because those are the things that are going to be rewarded by the majority.

JD: What makes good writing?

VTN: Oh, that's such a subjective question, and I think the subjective reaction for me is, What makes good writing is something that energizes me when I see it. I think that that is often different for every individual, but we all acquire a sense of taste.

For each of us, that sense of taste determines what we think is good. We're bored by certain things, stimulated by certain things. So, there's no right or wrong answer, you know?

Personally, I am provoked by writing in which I see that the language is really alive from the very first sentence.

I think about when I open a book and look at the first sentence or first paragraph. I can see, hopefully, the book in microcosm because the style, rhythm, word choice, and the very voice of the author are all present. It's like a seed in that first sentence or first paragraph, and if I don't like the seed, I'm probably not going to like the book. I mean, I can make a mistake here, but I need to be provoked from that very first sentence, that very first paragraph. If I feel that the language is inert or unoriginal or that the rhythm is flat, I'm not really interested in carrying on for 300 more pages of that.

When it comes to good writing, that is not to me a question of seriousness or literariness. I'm not a snob; I think that so-called genre writers can do exactly everything that I talked about, and so-called literary writers can fail in that respect. There are a lot of boring literary writers and a lot of really good so-called genre writers out there. So, this question of what is good is not a matter of snobbish literary values. It's a question about each individual writer within the constraints of the kind of genre that they picked for themselves, including the literary genre, what they do with that and whether they can make that genre original.

So, yes, I think originality is also part of what I'm looking for in terms of good writing. It's hard to discern originality if you haven't read deeply and widely. If you're a naive reader and then pick up a book, even the worst stuff can look great to you, which is why certain writers sell a lot of copies.

JD: I'm curious about what your media consumption is like. Do you have habits? Do you read the newspaper?

VTN: When I was growing up in the dark ages, there were only books, TV and radio, and magazines and newspapers. There were not even movies, really, because I could never go to the movies. Even back then, I read a lot of books, but I was also reading the newspapers. I was also watching a lot of TV—my dad was so upset by how much TV I was watching and would yell at me. He would unplug the TV and tape over the outlet, but that would not stop me from plugging the TV back in.

Somehow, out of all of that, I still became a writer, so I'm not snobbish about this issue of media consumption. I think that we live in a world of stories, and stories can come to us in many ways. Now, it is important, I think, if you want to be good as a storyteller, to pick a form and immerse yourself deeply, but that doesn't mean you have to exclude everything else that's out there. I think you can find powerful storytelling or writing in many different ways. Even Twitter is a form, and some people are really, really good at it, you know? I think I was decent at it—when I was on Twitter. In fact, Twitter did influence the last book that I finished. It's a nonfiction memoir built on fragments and short sentences and things like that. It was totally influenced by Twitter but also by poetry.

I try to read or watch anything that will provoke me because it captures my interest. I use an Excel sheet to track how much I'm reading—I'm probably doing like 90 books a year in both audio and written form. I also try to make sure that I'm reading as many women as I am men. Where I'm failing is I'm reading too many Americans and not enough non-Americans. That has to be corrected. I still like to watch TV, so I have Netflix and Amazon and Apple and all of that, and I try to watch TV shows that are doing interesting things and are entertaining but are also bringing new worlds to me. So, *Reservation Dogs* has been there recently, as have *Ramy* and *Westworld*. Regarding movies, most recently, there was *Dune*. I'm still reading newspapers, still get the physical *The New York Times*. I want to expose my son to all these forms of media so he knows that there are books and newspapers out there. I didn't have a library when I was growing up, while he has a library probably bigger than most adults have. He takes it for granted. I think that most of us take for granted that we have Facebook and Twitter, our laptops, our phones, and all of that. However, I think that for those of us with children, it's important to build and very consciously curate the kinds of things our kids get.

JD: Speaking of children, you co-authored the children's book *Chicken of the Sea* with your son, Elison. Young people's expectations of words and writing are so different from the world of publishing and academia that you often write about. What was that experience like?

VTN: Pure joy. It was completely unexpected; it was not me trying to be some stage dad, telling my son he had to write a book or anything. It's simply that my wife and I provided him with a house full of books, art, and music, all that kind of stuff. I think most kids are naturally creative—it's life that beats the creativity out of people. So, we got lucky—or he got lucky, too—that he created this little comic book, which a lot of kids do, but he just happened to have a dad who put it on Facebook, and I have a Facebook friend who I'd never met who was an editor who then turned that book into a real book. That's a sort of fairy-tale story, but I think the heart of the matter is that it doesn't matter if you get published or not. What really matters is that parents and children should have a relationship that allows for creativity and for parents to converse with their kids in this respect.

For me, part of the lesson from that experience was that childlike creativity is wonderful because it knows no boundaries and borders. As we grow older, we acquire boundaries and borders, rules and etiquette, concepts regarding what we shouldn't say or do. That's useful, obviously, but it can kill creativity, you know? And creativity, I think, is partly about seeing the world without any kind of limitation. If we bring it back directly to the question of literature, why does genre exist? Why do we have lines like that? And why do we talk about high and low or have rules that say you can or can't do certain things in the world of fiction?

After that, it became a father-son thing where we actually went on a book tour, and I took him to places like Washington, D.C. Earlier this year, we were in San Francisco and San Jose. This opens up a place where I can have a relationship with my son and do something with him that hopefully he'll remember positively. I think all parents should be seeking out that kind of opportunity.

JD: Your son is almost 10 now and you also have a younger daughter. Did watching them learn to speak change how you see words? You're a person that speaks various languages and thinks about words in a profound way. I imagine teaching language to someone that's learning how to be a person has to be a totally different experience.

VTN: I always had the idea that, in general, it's important not to talk down to kids. I talk to him [Ellison] like he's capable of understanding very serious things and serious words, and I think that's important because I think children can understand that. I don't know why parents go around talking down to their kids or adults go around talking down to kids, but it's a bad idea. I always assume that he and other children can rise to the challenge. As a result of that, we talk about serious political matters sometimes—he has opinions about Trump and racism, for example—because these ideas, the serious ideas of adults, will affect kids anyway. These ideas circulate non-verbally in people's households, or sometimes they circulate verbally—adults don't know that they're transmitting ideas and the kids are picking up on all kinds of stuff.

That's how children can be really vicious in the places where parents don't see things happening. There are plenty of stories about bullies and terrible things happening on playgrounds. Hopefully, that's not your kid, but maybe it is, and why do they do that? They do it because they learned it from adults, either the words or the behavior.

That's why I've always thought it was important to talk to my son about serious matters, because I want him to be an empathetic, caring, responsible person who's aware of how history has shaped him. He knows about words like war and colonialism and refugees because this is what shaped his grandparents and parents and led to him.

Besides that, talking to him like he's a serious person, we also do things that involve language. We read a lot together, and oftentimes that's silly and fun stuff—his favorite series is *Diary of a Wimpy Kid*. However, reading children's literature with him has been informative for me because in the world of children's literature, not just *Diary of a Wimpy Kid* but *Dog Man*, for example, I've learned a lot: Break rules! Entertain people! He's laughing hysterically at a lot of these words. Why can't adults also laugh hysterically at the things that they read? *Dog Man* is stupid, but it's also literary with titles like *Fetch-22* and *For Whom the Ball Rolls*—this is, like, smart stuff. So, regarding the issue of language and education, I think it's also a mistake for adults to think it's a one-way street, that it's only adults who teach kids. It's also kids who continue to teach adults—not intentionally but through observing them and remembering who we were when we were children.

Finally, it was important for me to have children who are multilingual. I think it's a real disability for Americans to be monolingual—the majority are—so my kids are enrolled in French school. I would have put them in Spanish school, but the problem is that the state of multilingual education is terrible in this country. I couldn't get them into K-12 Spanish school, so we put them in French school because I could pay for that. I've been in situations in France, for example, where I've seen people—young teenagers—speak French and English as if they're natives in both languages. I can't tell the difference to other Americans. I want that for him. I want him to have that kind of fluency because I do think that it allows you to see the world in different ways when you can approach language in different ways. When I was writing *The Sympathizer*, I knew enough Vietnamese that I could look at it from the outside and look at English from the outside, and *The Sympathizer* is written as someone who approaches English from the outside—that's why, I think, the language in that book is so dense in a particular way. I wanted to make that language a very deliberately self-conscious language, and it was really rewarding for me that someone who is Vietnamese recently came up to me and said, "I feel that this was written in Vietnamese." The sentence structure, he said, was Vietnamese to him. That was really awesome for me to hear, that he could see that structure in there.

With *The Committed*, there are a lot of French jokes in there, and they came about because, you know, my kids are learning French and I took French in high school. Also, over the last few years, I've been taking it very seriously and learning it again because I want to keep up with my kids—I don't want them to speak a language I can't understand. In the case of *The Committed*, knowing French allowed me to make jokes in French that the French catch, as well, which is awesome.

JD: I have some questions about community because writing is very lonely. You've spoken about ethnicity and automatically being part of a collective for that reason. What are the virtues of belonging to a collective and certain literary lineages?

VTN: Yeah ultimately, the writer is left alone in a room, so you do have to confront that solitude. There's no way of getting out of that, and for some writers, that's the world they want to inhabit completely, you know? So, more power to them. You can't really change a writer's personality. However, collectivity is important in a couple of different ways. In one way, it's important in the sense you're talking about, which is the need for some writers to actually have a physical community, to know that there are other people like them out there. Many of us need that kind of affirmation, whether it's knowing this in a sort of idealistic sense—we've read other writers like us, we know they exist and that's awesome—or actually forming communities that we can participate in physically. Of course, if you're a part of the majority, that ecosystem already exists for you—you go to a writer's residency, even go to New York City where you can hang out with other writers that you can assume are white. You take that for granted. For those of us who are not white, we have to build those communities, and I think it's a very important act because what it says is that writing is not only about the individual achievement and individual advancement. In fact, we can help each other along the way.

This, to me, is so important because when you are a part of the majority, you don't necessarily need that group, because there will be people like you who will recognize you and will give you that helping hand. If you're a so-called minority, that's very unlikely to happen. There's not going to be that famous editor out there or that famous professor who will reach down and pull you up. Therefore, we have to do it for ourselves, and we have to push each other up rather than have someone pull us. There are a lot of examples of that in terms of writers and collectives in the history of writers of color in the United States. Now, if we come from a group in which those collective leads have not yet existed, like for us Vietnamese people, then some of us have to take the initiative and start that on our own, which is what my friends and I have done.

We started off as young, idealistic writers in our 20s, looking around and seeing that there weren't enough Vietnamese voices out there and thinking maybe we needed to have a group of writers and artists that would provide the community, organize open mics, organize meetings, and give people an audience. That's exactly what happened, and from that little seed, 25 years later we have a 501c3 with a multi-hundred-thousand-dollar budget. It was done out of just sheer collective will and voluntary work, and now we have paid employees and staff. So, I think anybody, any group of people, can do that, but obviously it's a tax. It's a literal tax on our time because in addition to writing, now we do this as well. It's unfair. Well, there's no way of getting around it. Unfortunately, that's what it means to build a collective. I think back to those writers who are not a part of these kinds of things; they just want to sit in their rooms and write. If they go out into the world and are successful and say, "I'm just a writer," I'm personally offended by that, because they are completely unaware of how much work has already gone into creating a world where they could just be a writer.

So, if you're the genius who's been sitting in the room by yourself, and you publish your first book, and you're Chicana or you're Asian American or whatever, and you suddenly become the big thing and you're like, "I just did it by myself," that's so untrue. The world has been prepared for you by all these other collectives and struggles and so on that have taken place, that have prepared the world so that it would even recognize what an Asian American writer is. One hundred years ago, that poor person who was the writer sitting alone in a room emerged as an early Chinese American writer. No one knew what to do with that person, because the world hadn't been prepared for that person.

I think it's important for writers of color—minorities or minority writers—to understand that they're never just an individual writer. They are to the extent that they're sitting alone in a room, but once they go out into the world, they are not just an individual writer, and they should recognize that either they need the support of other people or their individual success has already been enabled by the social and/or political struggles of other writers that have gone before them.

JD: There is a lot of talk about the importance of elevating "marginalized voices" or "unheard voices" in the literary world and beyond, which opens the ethnic writer to larger audiences. However, I wonder about something you said in another interview with *The Washington Post*: whether greater visibility is similar to the skills immigrants develop in the process of assimilation—the mental elasticity in how they see themselves and others, which you explore in your books. Do you think the experience of seeing oneself through various perspectives translates to specific skills in writing as well?

VTN: I think so, and I think even if we look at writers of the so-called majority, they may be part of the majority, but in their own worlds, the way they grew up and all of that, I think they've probably experienced otherness as individuals—you know, alienation and "outsiderness." Something unique about their upbringing or background has made them sensitive to the inside of the outside, whether it's the inside and outside of language or the inside and outside of social relations of various kinds. I think literary writers are inevitably people who feel uncomfortable in some way in relation to either language or social relations, but those are individual circumstances. For an immigrant or refugee or writer of color or so-called minority, not only do we feel individually out of sorts, but we are collectively out of sorts because it's imposed on us. That's the big difference, right?

That's also the big difference when it comes to identity. If you're part of the majority, your identity is an individual identity, and you can take it or leave it, you can be ethnic or not depending on your choice. However, if you're a racialized minority, you have no choice. It's imposed on you, so I think that for those of us on whom various kinds of identities are imposed because of historical conditions and circumstances, we do have a different relationship with both the inside and outside of a particular moment. Because of the collective nature of that imposition, the force of that does transform my understanding of what otherness and inclusion might mean, and I think that manifests itself in terms of writing when it comes to the choices that we make about who and what we write about. Inevitably, if you're a so-called minority writer, it's political. Even when we speak about the people that you write about, to write as an Asian American is political because you picked a group that's already marked in the larger society. Of course, to not write about Asian Americans is also political because then it becomes, Why are you not writing about Asian Americans? If you're writing about an unmarked population, it turns into, Who is that population? Are they white or are they not white? So, it's that condition that is imposed on you and that, again, is not fair, but it's a key issue that marks us differently than it does white people, because if white people write about white people, it's not an explicit, political choice. It's just something that happens to be normal. If you're an Asian American writing about an Asian American, however, it is normal, but it's also political at the same time, because you can't separate the literature from the larger politics of the society.

I think that a very basic awareness of the imposition of identities and the fact that even things that should not be political are political must inevitably shape an immigrant or refugee writer's awareness of themselves. Does it make them more elastic? If I said that, I think that it could, but you can't generalize these things as an inevitability, because there are a lot of non-elastic immigrants and refugees too. However, it gives you the opening that you can walk through to choose to be elastic—

to choose to be more entrepreneurial, for example. They can choose to be more experimental, and, again, not every writer makes that choice, but the door has been opened for them to see that that choice could be an option.

JD: As a writer, do you feel a responsibility to subject yourself to adventures and life experiences?

VTN: To adventures and life experiences? Oh, yeah. I think that it's absolutely necessary for me to have new experiences. However, it's important to identify what those experiences are, because when I was growing up reading about writers like Ernest Hemingway and Jack London, the idea was that to be a man and a manly writer or to be writer in general, one had to seek out adventure in foreign lands, test their manhood and strength and all of that kind of stuff. That could be true, but I don't think that's actually necessary. To become a mother is a life-changing experience that a man will never have. To be an immigrant or a refugee is a life-changing experience that the citizen who grew up in this country will never have. So, I think every experience is potentially a life-changing experience, even the most seemingly mundane or domestic things. To become a father was a life-changing experience. I didn't want it—to me, it was deeply terrifying, even though it's a very mundane thing. Therefore, the qualified answer is "absolutely." Yes, you need new adventures. You need new experiences, but even the most mundane and domestic things can be those experiences. Even changing a job can be that kind of experience: For me, I feel like I've exhausted the life of a professor. I don't think I can learn anymore from this job. I'd love to resign and retire and do something else. I would love to leave this country and live in another country for the next couple of decades, and I think that's one of the reasons why learning French has been important. That was an important experience—is an important experience—for me as a writer and as a human being to subject myself to humiliation through learning something.

For a lot of people, they get comfortable, they get authority in whatever it is that they're doing, and for a lot of people, they don't want to lose that authority and that comfort and stability. I think that's true for writers as well, and that's dangerous. I think that for me, my own project is to constantly feel like I'm learning something, but if you're going to learn something, you have to be a student, and to be a student when you're already a professor means you have to give up authority. Can you do that? Can you subject yourself to feelings of inadequacy, humiliation, embarrassment, vulnerability? This is what it means to learn stuff, however you choose to do it. It can be, again, as mundane as learning a new language, or it could be traveling to a foreign country and not as a tourist.

I think writers have so many opportunities to do these kinds of things, as every human being does, but it takes a little bit of courage to expose yourself to new things.

JD: Last question: Do you practice other forms of creative output besides writing?

VTN: Promoting other Vietnamese American diasporic artists and writers is helpful to me in the sense that it exposes me to new ideas, new stories that are out there. When I was growing up in the Vietnamese-refugee community, and I was looking at these very old people in their 30s and 40s telling their stories and stuff, I was like, "God, these stories are old and tired. When are you going to learn some new stories? Why are you trapped in the past?" Now, I'm older than those people were at that time, and I think that there are probably younger people looking at me, and I know this is happening: "Wow. Can you just think of a new story to talk about besides refugees and war?" And they are perfectly right in saying that. So, it's good for me to know that there are younger generations of writers who are concerned about totally different things. That goes back to the question about learning new stuff and having your own authority undermined or questioned and your view of the world put into relief. I think being a parent has been a bit of a creative endeavor in some ways. Therefore, I'm looking forward to being able to give up certain parts of my life. For instance, if I stop being a professor, that should open up more time to do other creative things. I would love to write a script for *The Sympathizer* TV series at some point. I'm not shutting myself off to other creative endeavors at this point, but right now, I just need to finish this Sympathizer Trilogy.

After Passing the Standardized Field Sobriety Test, I

Hannah Cohen

imagine the universe where I failed. Your apocryphal girl
        buzzing toward black yonder. There I am,
    alphabetizing gone opportunities. Other-me
in the passing driver's window, transparent.
          Uncaring. If doppelgängers exist, let me be
the amphibious one. A creature crosshatched
        between drought and bedroom. The cerebral sea
    aglow with heat. Another-me tempting myth
or mister. I live a stumbling odyssey of consequences
        disembodied. This dark voyage
without a chorus.

The First Time I Thought My Father Could Kill Me

Mimi Yang

After 李绅's 悯农二首

There was a heatwave making landfall
in Changsha. At his great uncle's farm
where we skipped stones like sorrows
flung across empty paddy fields, sank
our clean feet into the thick clay
of the canal, & joked about skinning cattle
to save them from summer. Our sweat
beading into rice like seeds into soil, dusk
piercing slumber. The poem we were
made to remember, of the farmer
who did not survive the harvest, now
sowing nations into our mouths. Here
at the table, I watch him feed the meat-
mouth dogs his chicken bones. I cannot
stop thinking of his hands, how they closed
over belts, how he softens them
now, stroking a muzzle glinting sharp
with teeth. After each meal, I sit with him
as he washes a sputtering carp, scrubbing
off scales & flesh until only a branch
of ribs remain, listening to his mother tell every lie
he was once struck for. *Oh*, I think, *this is how
I'll go*. Her pride reared by our silence, famine
forgiven by the seasons. A child, terror-stricken
& fleeing into fatherhood. My executioner, a loving
father silvered by rage, a root out of my reach.

In the Beginning, Forest
Hannah Marshall

A forest was painted onto the cinderblock wall
of my Sunday School room
where the office-bright lighting didn't extend. The sun
sat in the corner, metallic gold. And the forest
was with God. And the forest was God. The forest was real
when I reached my hand toward it. It was a pine forest,
a winter scene, very Narnian, and I could smell it,
could feel the cold on my fingers. The forest was with God
in the beginning, and I walked there,
where the seemingness of the world
and all the stories and symbols became forest, red needles
crackling on frozen moss. The sun could be stared into
because it was pure gold, and the sky was white as institution,
and the trees were uniform and spoke of pain
when the wind blew. In the beginning, the forest
was Sunday School, and my Sunday shoes were silty
and sturdy, and the forest held us children, and the songs
were the wind and the sparrows. In the beginning, love
was a forest, and the forest was a wild beast. In the beginning,
God was wild and unbound from onion-skin sheaves
and not shut in pine boxes and not taught with fire and blood.
In the beginning, the forest was thick with silence
and could not be named, but even then, I loved the words.

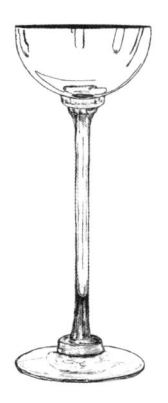

The Sinkhole

ADRIÁN PÉREZ

—

fiction

ON THE NIGHT MY HUSBAND, STEPHEN, AND HIS mistress drove off a cliff in Maine, a sinkhole opened in front of our house here in Florida, swallowing one neighbor's car and another's dog. The dog's owner, Tanya, said she heard a rumbling then felt its leash pull away like an anchor. *Imagine if I'd been holding it tight,* she said, *I'd be gone just like Buster.* As if her inch-long fingernails would let her hold anything tightly.

That morning, my husband told me he was leaving as I was laying out breakfast for our son, Jack. As I put down a pancake, he erupted with a flow of announcements: He had been having an affair with his assistant professor, they were leaving for a four-day trip to Maine, and our marriage was over. I kept looking down at the plate, impressed with my browning technique.

I could tell Stephen expected a fight, his slung jacket a shield to protect him from a flying dish or butter knife. For a few moments, we were a paused videotape, lines and static between us. I put down the spatula, filling the moment with a dramatic sigh while I thought of a reply. *Is your mother still coming?* was all I managed to say. He sighed, too, half as long but twice as potent.

His mother, Barbara, was coming in a week. She wasn't the mother-in-law you saw in movies: There was no snarky undertone, she didn't walk around checking surfaces for dust. But, she did resent me for taking her son from her, slipping in when her back was turned with my southern twang and crescent hips. Ironically, when I had Jack, I understood—all mothers are victims of theft eventually.

Stephen had it planned out: He'd call his mother to reschedule, tell Jack he was on a work trip, and, when he got back, explain three was becoming two. It was a shock but not a surprise—since our son's birth four years earlier, there'd been a shift in allegiances. Love with my husband had been bidirectional, a thing passed between us. But, Jack was a well I filled with every breath, flinging pieces of myself into an endless hole that never gave back. I don't know how any marriage was expected to survive a bomb like that.

* * *

The sinkhole opened around 10 p.m. while most of the block was asleep except for Tanya, who was walking Buster. Gossip had it she was coming back from a rendezvous with a married man named Bill, a neighbor who bought Tanya the dog so they could hook up while he was walking his. I met him once at a neighborhood function: balding, doughy, spacious teeth, laugh a deflating tire. But, his eyes were kind—a light that outshone the rest.

I was standing outside Jack's bedroom when I heard the boom from the sinkhole. He'd made a fuss about going to bed, as if he sensed the unraveling of his family through the extra ice cream at dinner. After he fell asleep, I stayed looking at the family photos taped to his door. We'd need a knife to cut Stephen out.

Tanya's screams were an even louder explosion. Otherworldly. Running out, I expected to see her wrestling a demon to the ground. Instead, a black lake was between us, like someone had taken an eraser to the street. At the edge was Tanya, on her knees, crying into the darkness for Buster.

As I got closer, a few neighbors materialized. There was Mike calling 911; his wife, Carol, directing people to stay away, arms out like a hallway monitor. Judy and Ed stumbled forward, mouths black holes like the one before us. I waited for Stephen to join before remembering he was with a woman who wasn't me.

We had loved nighttime adventures. Our second date was an evening picnic in Loblolly Woods. We'd taken two bites of a baguette when we decided to get sex out of the way. If it was bad, we could blame the swamp. If it was good, we could blame the swamp when it wasn't as good later. As Stephen was doing a striptease, he accidentally tossed his keys—we spent half an hour looking for them, working as a team. That night, seeds for a future together were planted.

Sirens from the Gainesville police were circling like birds, and I felt alone for the first time since Stephen's blowup. Something like this was exactly the kind of thing you'd want to talk over with a partner. Showing Jack wouldn't be the same thing. He'd just want to see how deep the hole was, toss things in to test the depth.

Other neighbors were coming out in their robes, looking at the police and city workers flocking to our little nuisance. Some cast judgmental glances at Tanya as if she had fucked the hole into existence. It occurred to me I was the insignificant other or whatever they called the ones cheated on. Did that make Tanya my enemy by proxy?

We'd never interacted much. In truth, she was talked more *about* than *to*, defined by the whispers of others. Tanya was in marketing in some form or another, making people feel inadequate without whatever she was selling.

* * *

When my phone rang after midnight, I thought it was Stephen calling to apologize, telling me he was on his way back with flowers and a promise. But, the cascade of words coming from my phone were from a stranger's lips: a narrow road, a lot of rain, a dangerous cliff. The man who wasn't my husband waited for a response.

I think you've got the wrong number, I said.

I'm sorry, ma'am, I don't, he replied with the emotion of a lamp.

Stephen is a common name; it's a mistake.

I understand it's a shock.

But he's a good driver. He wouldn't let that happen.

If you're not from around here, these roads can be tricky.

He's. A. Good. Driver.

I know this is hard to hear.

It's not hard, because you're joking.

We don't joke about these things.

My jaw locked up, tongue paralyzed so all I could do was bark like a seal hoping to be thrown a treat. I'd never thought about Stephen dying without me; it felt so lonely. Was it lonely for him?

Was he with anyone? I finally spit out. Then came a pause big enough to dwarf the sinkhole outside.

Yes, ma'am. We're notifying her family as well.

I hung up and turned off my phone when he started talking details. I got a bottle of wine from downstairs along with a few Sominex tablets and gulped both like I was twenty-one again.

***

In the morning, Jack's head appeared at my bedroom door, smiling like Stephen, a mini version of my dead husband asking to come into bed. Was it the mother or the lover that said yes?

He came in, put his head on my shoulder, and looked up, curling into the space between us. It's like he knew the preciousness of childhood was fleeting.

Can we call Daddy and say good morning?

He said it so casually, I choked.

Stephen dying was a meteor going so fast the air hummed. I couldn't protect us, so I turned my eyes to the ground, focusing on every blade of grass, knowing when it landed it would take us both. I just didn't want to know when.

Honey, he called when you were asleep. He said good morning and he loves you.

Okay, we can call when he's not at work, Jack conceded.

I told him to put on clothes so I could show him something he'd never seen before. While he was changing, I turned on my phone; eight voicemails from the same two Maine numbers were waiting. It was easy to delete them.

At 8:27, the theme from *Amélie* started playing—my cue to give Stephen a ten-minute warning for work. We'd dance to that song in our kitchen, knocking things over, neither very graceful. I had loved that about us, the way we embraced things we weren't good at because we weren't good at them *together*. Sometimes when I was mad at him, I'd imagine us awkwardly dancing and fall newly in love, the fresh kind that nips at your ear.

Jack yelped and ran as soon as he saw the sinkhole, stopping when he got to the caution tape and sad-eyeing me to walk faster. Neighbors gathered in clusters, holding their coffee cups and looking at the sinkhole like a stain that needed washing. It was curb-to-curb wide. The bottom was a gray mist with the hint of a red mound—my neighbor's Porsche, a sporty thing he bought when he turned fifty.

I thought of Stephen's car at the bottom of a cliff. Him and his lover in the wreckage, facing each other, eyes open in shock, holding hands. What were they listening to as they flew over? A podcast? Music? Were his last thoughts of me?

I felt a warmth on my leg: a leak, something escaping.

Mommy, you're peeing! Jack jumped back from me like *I* was a hole opening. Fifteen pairs of eyes landed on me, the yellow circle at my feet more interesting than the big black one.

Quiet! I snapped at Jack, but he was still dancing around as if on fire. I grabbed his wrist and bolted back to the house, hands tightening with each step. I heard squeals of pain behind me but didn't take my eyes off the front door, my shield.

Inside, he was sniffling and looking at his hands. The smell of piss between us was the only communication for a few seconds. I was embarrassed, angry, ashamed. I tried the role of repentant mother.

I'm sorry, honey.

He shrugged, nodded slightly.

Can you go upstairs and get Mommy a towel?

He turned, leading with his shoulder, little legs taking wide steps up the stairs, just like Stephen would. For a moment, I thought Jack was mocking me.

My phone rang, a Maine number—I sent it to voicemail. After a minute, a notification popped up. I stepped into the backyard to listen. The sunlight felt protective, and if things got too intense, I could chuck the phone into the bushes, let the worms sort things out.

It was a woman this time, the tone in her voice a sugary revulsion. Apparently, not answering your phone after your spouse died wasn't acceptable. My faux pas.

Hello, this is Officer Gellman from the Maine State Police. We've tried contacting you several times. There's a lot we need to discuss regarding the passing of your husband. You can ask to talk to me or Officer Ingersoll, but it's important we speak as soon as possible. Thank you.

In the sliding glass door, my reflection looked like a dress swinging from a wire hanger. Jack was just beyond, towel in hand, head positioned right next to my hip. His eyes and mouth were three craters I couldn't see the depths of.

The house phone rang, a remnant from another era. We only used cellphones now, but Stephen had said he felt odd not having one around. Jack ran over and picked up. I heard *Hi, Grandma!* fly from his throat. Barbara. I rushed into the house.

Daddy's at work, Jack pronounced. *She's here*, he said, handing the phone to me.

Barbara? My heart tried collapsing; my chest tried to catch it.

Sorry to bother you, but I left a few messages with Stephen, and he hasn't gotten back to me.

He hadn't called her, she was still coming. I was at the bottom of a mountain, watching the first sections of snow come loose.

He's at a conference for a few days, I stammered.

Who'll pick me up from the airport? she said after a few moments. I hated her for asking that.

We'll figure it out. I have to go; something's on the stove.

The phone fell off the hook when I tried hanging up, rejecting my lies. It crashed to the floor, skidded next to Jack, who looked like someone had dropped a dead body at his feet. When he reached to pick it up, I told him to leave it in a razor voice. He whimpered and ran upstairs.

Walking past the living room window, I saw Tanya standing at the end of our driveway. I could see why someone would buy her a cover dog. She was fit—big boobs that were probably fake but looked real enough to question and an ass that looked carved. Every time you saw her, she had the air of someone who had just finished having the best sex. We met eyes for a second, the invitation she needed.

BOOTH

I opened the door as she was walking up, getting a whiff of the urine I had yet to wipe off.

Sorry about Buster, Tanya, I started.

Thanks. It was just so sudden, I couldn't hold on.

Well, that was probably for the best. Too tight and you might've fallen, too. Silver linings, I guess.

She nodded and gave me a half-abandoned smile. *Jack looked excited to see the hole. Stephen not interested?*

He's at a conference in Ohio.

He's always leaving for something. He go with anyone?

Her eyes had an expectant look, too excited for the moment.

No, just himself.

Well, make sure to keep an eye out; you don't want him falling.

Stephen?

Jack. You know how boys are.

* * *

The rest of the morning was filled with artful dodging every time Jack asked to call his father. I wouldn't let him finish, deflecting the question with a cookie, a carton of juice, a growl. I wanted to pack him away until I was ready, put him in a box. The next minute felt exhausting. The next week felt crippling. The rest of my life felt horrifying.

He'd had enough of my evasion after lunch.

I want to call Daddy right now, he said, rooting himself like a 500-pound boulder.

I caved in. The phone trembled as I pressed his number and it started ringing, afraid a stranger would answer. Afraid Stephen would.

It went straight to voicemail, an echo of another life. I remembered when he set up the message, fretting over coming across as too informal for his colleagues but too distant for his students. In the end, he sounded like someone who wanted it to be over: the phone call, the message, our marriage.

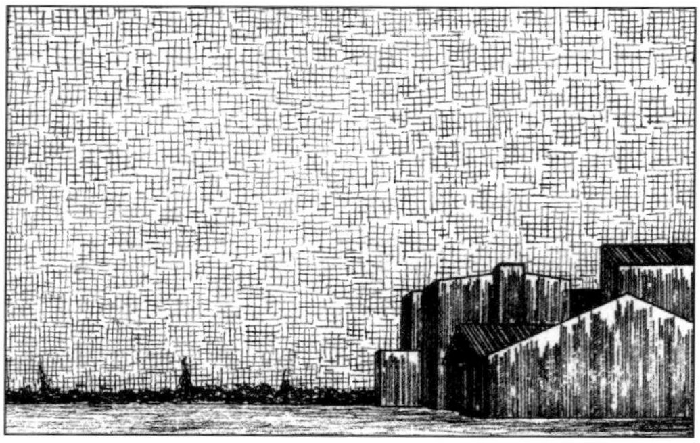

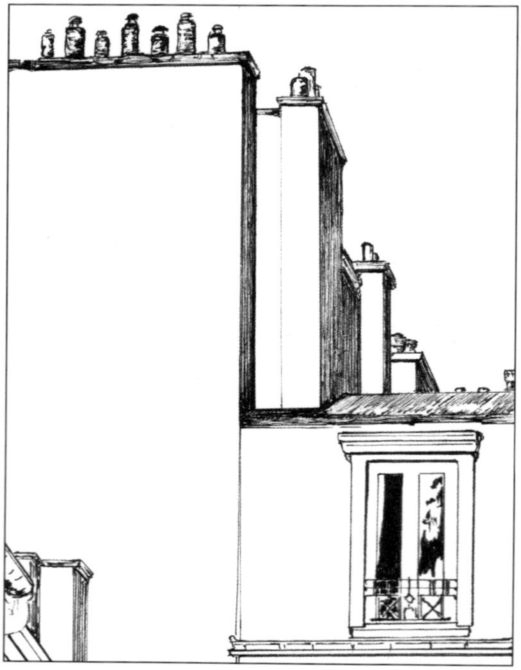

Mommy, you're biting yourself. Jack shook me lightly.

I wiped red streaks against my hand. They looked like escaping ghosts.

Let's leave a message together, okay?

I love you Daddy I miss you Daddy there's a big hole call back. I didn't add anything.

***

Cleaning up after lunch, I snarled at Jack so much he cowered like a rain-soaked dog. Every time he made a sound—loading the dishwasher, closing a drawer—he looked at me with a simmering dread. I didn't care. It kept him from talking.

Mid-afternoon, I got a call from a neighbor—I had forgotten about a play date for Jack with her son Trevor. We couldn't get there fast enough.

Stephen had never liked this couple—Martha and Dillon—saying they were too low-class for us. I'd remind him I was descended from tenant farmers, as low as it got for some. He'd say I was different, of course, but I sometimes felt his love for me was conditional—that if I pulled out a jar of Miracle Whip, he'd pack his bags.

Martha kept asking about Stephen as I was leaving. She had a crush on him; once, when he was featured in the local paper, she kept the article on their fridge for months. Dillon worked at a demolition company, and there was always grime loitering on his face—a biology professor at the university was probably exotic. I both *did* and *didn't* understand her fascination. Sure, Stephen was witty and intelligent, but Dillon was sexy and primal in a way my husband never was.

I finally told her I had to meet a friend, which got Jack's attention.

Mommy, who are you seeing?

Just a friend, honey.

Can I come?

No. Have fun with Trevor.

I don't want to.

At that, he clamped onto my leg. Martha tried helping.

Jack, Trevor got a new truck. It's pretty cool.

Jack held tighter. I asked Martha to give us a minute. She ushered Trevor—who looked like he didn't give a shit either way—into the kitchen.

I need to go by myself, I hissed. *Stay here and play for a while.*

It hurts, he whined.

I had not realized I was grabbing his arm. I loosened my grip but didn't let go, punctuating each word with a squeeze.

Stay with Trevor.

How long?

Until I say so.

The concern on his face would've broken a better woman's heart.

* * *

A surveyor was taking measurements of the sinkhole when I got home. He said the Porsche would be pulled out, and anything else down there—trash, pieces of asphalt, Buster—would be covered up, swept under the rug by a fifty-ton broom. Around the perimeter of the sinkhole, the city put "No Dumping" signs.

The house felt like the insides had been scraped out and only skin remained. Every time a thought of Stephen or Jack slithered into my head, I squeezed it out by humming a song or reading a book out loud. This was supposed to be my time; couldn't they do that for me?

Different Maine numbers kept calling. I chuckled, imagining the police thinking they'd fool me, twirling villainous mustaches with each call. Sometimes, they left messages. Always, I deleted them.

While taking a bath, I sank under the water, watching the world dissolve above me, disappointed when I hit bottom. A muffled howl like a coyote's lapped my ears. I thought it might be Stephen crying out for me, for the wrong he'd done. It repeated itself. Again. When I came up for air, Jack's voice told someone to leave a message.

Hello, this is Officer Gellman. We've left several messages on your cell phone. It's important you call us.

I cut the cords of the phones we had in the house. I also threw away the tapes in the answering machines. It was outdated tech; we needed to move on.

***

Jack was so shaken when I picked him up, I offered a pizza party as an apology.

He didn't ask to call Stephen, and in return I let him stay up well past his bedtime, pretending to wrestle with the idea. I would've let him watch TV forever if it meant not talking about his father. I'd be a dusty old maid, he a middle-aged mama's boy, as we watched Bugs Bunny escape death for the 10,000th time.

They even slept like each other, mouths open as if mid-sentence. I'd tease Stephen that spiders would lay eggs in his mouth sleeping like that. Once, he pretended to convulse and "threw up" candy eggs all over our bed, laughing the entire time. That was before the egg that came out of me made us both sick.

After I brought Jack up to bed, I heard a clank outside. Tanya was at the edge of the sinkhole, taking things from a shopping bag and softballing them into it. I stepped out, intrigued.

Hiding evidence? I joked.

It's a funeral for Buster. I'm sending him off with his toys.

You're not worried about getting caught throwing stuff down there?

Caught by who, these judgmental assholes? She broadly gestured.

There was acid in her voice. I must've looked shocked—her tone softened a little.

Sorry, I had a talk with one of our lovely neighbors earlier, she continued.

About what? I played dumb.

Oh, come on.

I guess I figured you didn't know we knew.

Because I'd stop seeing Bill if I did?

Well, yeah.

I don't care what people think.

What about his wife? Don't you care what you're doing to her?

I'm not "doing" anything to her.

You are. You're fucking her husband.

Oh, come on, you know better. Fucking someone else isn't the first sign of a broken marriage, it's the last.

I started to reply, but the look Tanya heaved at me was a warning. She threw one final toy in, waved dismissively, then blended into the darkness. I turned back to the house.

The pulse of red lights from the barricades was a heartbeat against the siding, the front door an aorta waiting for blood to rush in. Or a person—a drifter, a burglar. Maybe worse. Walking upstairs, I left the door open, praying for whoever accepted my invitation to spare me from the days ahead.

***

The next morning, a construction worker stopped by, saying the sinkhole would be filled the following day. The street had been inspected and our house had been deemed safe. *Not for me*, I said.

Closing the door, I heard hesitant steps approaching, causing a wild rage to tear through me. *Let's go to the woods then get some ice cream*, I said before the words "daddy" or "phone" could leave Jack's lips. He suggested we find a pretty spot and video chat with Stephen. I told him he had meetings all day.

Barbara called my cell phone as Jack was changing. She must have been desperate to call me directly; the only times she did was to plan surprises for Stephen. I let it ring; no message ever arrived. There was nothing for me to say no to.

Walking to the car, Jack ran to the sinkhole without saying a word. I thought he was going to jump in, join his father in some faraway hole. In the seconds before he reached the edge, I imagined a double funeral, selling the house, moving to Paris.

Jack, stop!

The sound piercing the air didn't come from my throat but someone else's. I looked around.

Neighbors were gaping at me in disgust; I waited for one to say something, anything. Jack tossed an apple into the sinkhole and came back to the car, giving me a light hug. I sneered at the world.

I wanted to give Buster a snack so he wouldn't get hungry, he told me with the purest sincerity.

Driving to the outskirts of the city, we passed a funeral home. At a stoplight, I watched a sea of black suits and dresses flowing inward, envious of the people diving into their sorrow. My hands caressed the steering wheel like I was consoling it. I crossed the meridian and parked in the lot.

Mommy, why did we stop? Jack asked.

See those people? Something bad happened to their friend, and they're going inside to talk about it.

Do you know her?

I did. We're going inside for a little bit.

It was a woman who had died; she looked about my age. Her name was Deborah Fields; the photo they used for the poster was the kind you got at a Walmart studio. She was wearing too much makeup—her eyes looked bruised rather than sultry—and behind her a forest was crying autumn leaves. Her photo brought out tears, ones I could disguise in the surrounding grief.

For our first Christmas as husband and wife, Stephen and I sent out photo cards. We went to a studio that hadn't been updated since the

70s. The photographer kept saying, *Oh, yeah, that's it. Nice, nice!* as we got sillier and sillier with our poses. When we were leaving, he said he also did boudoir photography and handed me his business card. Stephen took it and winked, saying *he'd* be back. I couldn't wait to fuck him when we got home.

Jack and I were very underdressed, so I plopped us in the back row. Up front was Deborah's open casket, fifty or sixty people in line to say goodbye. Both of us looked around awkwardly.

Is that your friend? He pointed to the casket.

Yes, her name was Deborah.

Is she asleep?

Sometimes, people get so hurt or so sick they don't wake up. Ever.

They can't shake her?

No, and that's why everyone is so sad. They have to say goodbye forever.

Are we going to say goodbye?

In college, a friend talked me into taking an improv class. The only thing I remembered was the teacher telling us comedy was all about committing to the bit.

Sure, I replied.

The same person that did Deborah's makeup in life seemed to have done it in death. Still, she looked pretty, with a perfect nose and laugh lines around her mouth that looked earned. Jack looked up at me for guidance, expecting me to say something or kiss her forehead like he had seen others do.

Say goodbye, Mommy, he said like a dare.

I bent over and kissed Deborah's clammy cheek, whispering the few words from the Lord's Prayer I remembered. Jack raised his arms, and I held him like Superman over her. He loudly said *Bye!* and kissed her forehead several times, then her mouth for several moments. There was a gasp behind us. Someone said *Ewww*.

Back in our seats, a woman asked how I knew Deborah; I said we'd been friends since high school.

Did she ever mention suicide? she asked.

No, I said, *but these things come out of nowhere. All it takes is one thing to push us over the edge.*

I would have considered it if it wasn't for Jack. Then again, if it wasn't for Jack, maybe Stephen wouldn't have left. I looked at my little anchor, legs swinging off the edge of the pew like he was ready to jump, thinking how a drop of doubt could poison an ocean.

Deborah's mother got up to speak, a bubble of emotions around her. Jack put his hand on my lap, giving my thigh a squeeze like his father used to do when I was anxious. Startled, I shoved it away, telling him to be still until the funeral was over. He looked like a rejected lover.

In the parking lot, Jack grabbed my wrist and spun me around. *Mommy, we can go home. You're too sad*, he said in a protective tone, cupping his chin with his hand—Stephen's pose when deciding something.

I slapped his hand away, yelled at him to stop pretending to be his father. His eyes started to water and his lips quivered; when I tried apologizing, he pushed me away. A few friends of Deborah looked ready to call child services.

I want Daddy.

He's at work, he can't talk.

Call him, he screamed so loud I'm sure Stephen heard.

Fine.

I took out my phone, dialed Stephen's number, and smashed it against Jack's ear so hard he pulled away. I pushed his head back with my other hand, feeling plastic against bone. We gave each other defiant looks.

Daddy! Where are you? Jack yelled into the phone when voicemail picked up.

He can't hear you.

At that, he became a sobbing mess that fell onto the asphalt, pounding it with his fists. Not his worst tantrum, but it was up there.

Jack, I told you he's busy with work, I said.

Is he mad at me?

Who *was* Stephen mad at? When he told me he was leaving, he said he'd been unhappy for a while, but what does that mean? Six months? A year? Four?

We didn't have sex for months after our son was born. I was breastfeeding, and my body felt like it was Jack's, like intercourse would defile the temple I had built for him. Every time Stephen tried to initiate something, I retreated. Eventually, he gave up trying, and I had assumed the late nights in his office were spent masturbating.

When we finally did have sex again, it was on his birthday, and we fumbled through it like first-timers. Afterward, as we lay staring at the ceiling, he said, *Thanks for the pity fuck.* I didn't correct him.

I picked Jack up off the ground and draped him over me, his head nestling into my neck, mucus and water rubbing into my skin. As I was putting him in the car seat, my phone rang. It was Barbara. I accidentally hit answer instead of ignore. I steeled myself.

Hi, Barbara.

What is going on? No one is answering my phone calls. Is everything okay?

We're fine. Just busy, and I'm not feeling well.

You don't sound well. Is Stephen back?

No. Not for a few days yet.

I'm coming tomorrow. I have a friend who's a travel agent; she can help.

We're fine. Stephen will be back soon.

I'll take a taxi from the airport, she said with the finality of a guillotine.

***

Barbara coming meant telling her about Stephen, which meant telling Jack. I decided to take us to Daytona Beach, the edge of the continent. Maybe further.

The idea of driving to the coast birthed another idea. While Jack was taking his afternoon nap, I called Martha and asked to speak to Dillon. Her tone changed from friendly neighbor to protective wife. I imagined her right up against his ear, listening in to catch us making secret plans.

I explained Stephen was too busy to call and it was really upsetting Jack. Dillon said it was natural for a boy to miss his father, with which I agreed vehemently. Then I went in for the ask.

I know this sounds strange, but would you mind calling and pretending you're Stephen? Just to say hi to Jack.

What?

Just for a minute. It would mean so much to him.

You want me to lie to the boy? I had no idea Dillon was so moralistic.

Not lie, just pretend. He's really heartbroken. A few words, that's all.

He put the phone on mute, probably telling Martha what a bad mother I was. This would get me a couple hours, maybe days, of quiet. I didn't care.

Please, I'll pay you, I said into the silence.

No need for that. Okay, but just to say hi. And we tell Stephen when he gets back. I don't want anything weird between us.

***

When he called, Jack was leery at first, asking if "Stephen" had a cold. Dillon did well with improvisation, saying his allergies had kicked in. I was feeling smug until Jack wanted to make it more than a quick hello.

Daddy, we saw our favorite cartoon.

How nice.

It's the great . . . Jack started. Stephen would always finish with, "Galactic Defender, villains beware!"

Pumpkin, Charlie Brown? Dillon said.

No, Galactic Defender. Remember?

Oh, yeah. Of course. Hurrah, Galactic Defense!

Daddy, you're being silly; that's not what he says.

I chimed in. *Honey, your father has to work. Say goodbye.*

Pérez   51

Goodbye, Daddy. I love you, Jack yelled.

I love you too, Trevor, was Dillon's response. Understandable.

Daddy, I'm Jack.

Of course! I love you too, Jack. Be a good boy and listen to your mother.

Then there was silence. Jack stared at the phone for a few seconds.

I think Daddy's sick, he said.

I shooed him into the backyard to play while I packed clothes. We'd leave after dinner to avoid traffic and be at Daytona Beach in less than two hours. If Jack asked any questions, I'd tell him we were going to meet Stephen then delay, delay, delay.

Jack and I had traveled alone before while Stephen stayed home since his schedule was so rigid. People warned me having a kid was a tether you couldn't break free from, but Jack was my escape. Whatever guilt I felt about leaving Stephen behind was absorbed by my son.

I was loading up the car when an hourglass shadow fell on the ground next to me, footsteps following in a hurried pattern.

You going somewhere? Tanya sounded grave.

If this is about last night, I'm sorry. Things are stressful right now.

I know. Stephen talk to you?

I slammed the trunk. *Look. I know you think you're the expert on adultery. Stay out of this.*

It's just that I don't like keeping other people's secrets. When I caught them, I told him he had to tell you.

Caught them? Were they here?

She nodded. My stomach fell to the other side of the world. *No, no, no,* I breathed, backing away.

I know you think it's your—

My hands went to my ears, blocking out Tanya and the whole goddamn world.

Turn around. Go away. Don't come back, I yelled.

She wouldn't stop, so I kicked her, landing blows to her thigh, all the while covering my ears and singing to drown her out. Tanya seemed keenly aware of the spectators up and down the street and backed off.

I looked at our house, which had gone from white to gray, safe to sinister. They had been here. Fucked here. Laughed at me here. I needed to get rid of his treachery.

I ran inside, locked the door to the backyard, and began emptying his dresser, closet, every backpack or briefcase he had. Into garbage bags went Stephen's clothes. Christmas cards and Valentine's Day gifts. His diplomas and photos.

Jack asked to be let in, tapping lightly on the door then pounding when I didn't answer. *Mommy, Mommy!* was blasting from his mouth, bouncing off the glass, the house, my head. Only his bedroom was left to purge.

Stephen and I didn't want a typical gendered one. There would be no firetruck wallpaper, no blue-colored furniture. He suggested we paint it our favorite colors since we'd be spending so much time in there. I had felt so partnered with him in those small moments, and now here I was on my hands and knees, looking at evidence of his cheating.

What I found wasn't as scandalous as a used condom or a pair of bunched-up panties. It was a bright pink hairband under Jack's bed. You don't expect the ordinary to level you.

When I was finished and finally let Jack in the house, he said, *I hate you I hate you I hate you* so many times it sounded like he was sneezing. Dinner was a partly frozen chicken pot pie he dared not complain about.

***

Just after midnight, I went outside and grabbed the first of seven garbage bags I had left on the side of the house. It felt as heavy as Jack. As I approached the edge of the sinkhole, I stopped, feeling the need to make a speech.

I was happy; I thought you were, too. Whose fault was this? I miss you. Goodbye.

The bag didn't even fall with a satisfying thud, only a rustle of plastic and some indiscriminate snapping. No lights went on in any houses, no one poked their head through curtains. I was alone.

The last bag ripped just as I got to the edge. Staring up at me was a photo of us at our engagement party—I was talking to a friend, and Stephen was looking at me with the faith of a newborn. I kicked it into the darkness.

I sat on the edge with my feet dangling into the emptiness. Only one thing was left: my wedding ring. Into the mouth it went, making a ting as it hit something. I was so tired, I didn't hear Jack approach.

Mommy?

What are you doing? Go back inside.

What are you *doing?*

I'm throwing away trash.

Was it too much for the trash cans?

It was.

He sat next to me, kicking his feet like he was on a swing. In the moonlight, his profile was exactly like Stephen's: the same sloping brow, beautiful Roman nose, fuller-than-average lips. No matter what I threw away, no matter how deep the hole, I would see my husband every day for the rest of my life.

I put my hand on his back. I could feel bones through his skin; the ridges of his spine felt like escalators moving forward. His body was directing me.

No one would be surprised. A curious child. A front door left carelessly unlocked. A terrible double tragedy. Maybe father and son would land in the same position.

Jack filled the negative space between us. *I love you Mommy* fell into the dark.

***

The sinkhole was filled over the next few days, during which time I sent Jack to stay with my mother. When she asked why, I told her Stephen and I had gotten in a fight. When she asked for the real reason, I said I was feeling confused. When she kept pressing me, I told her I wasn't sure I could keep Jack safe. The silence that followed was the most honest time I'd ever spent with her.

I told Barbara everything, and instead of visiting us, she flew to Maine to pick up Stephen's body, angry *I* abandoned *him*. When she insinuated it was my fault he cheated, I told her to crawl into the coffin with her son. I can count on both hands the times we spoke after that.

With Jack, it was different; I kept Stephen's memory pure as a final act of love. He knew it was a car accident. He knew he was in Maine. He knew his father was never coming back. And that was it.

He slept in my bed for months, leaving space between us in case a body miraculously appeared in the emptiness, closing the gap each night until there was none. Eventually, we stopped listening for the front door to open.

Sometimes, when I walk across the spot where the sinkhole was, I feel a pull toward the bottom, like everything I tossed in is calling for me. On nights when I can't sleep, I'll go out and lay over it, arms open like an embrace. Jack is terrified, convinced the slightest movement or agitation will cause the hole to open up again. He's not wrong.

Asopao

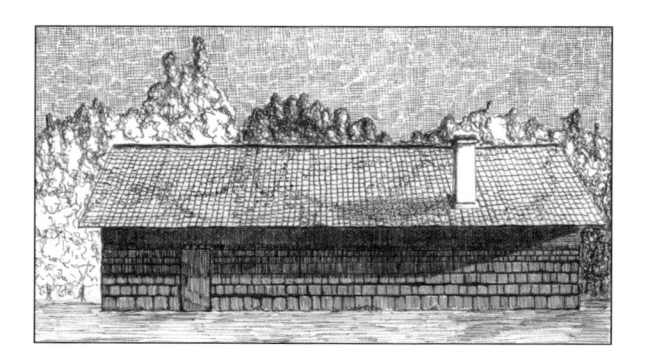

JERILYNN AQUINO

—

nonfiction

THIS IS MY FIRST WINTER since moving to Oklahoma, and like any Puerto Rican needing comfort, I make asopao de pollo. The closest recipe to the one I know calls for a whole chicken, cut into pieces.

Adobo, cilantro, short-grain rice. A chicken, nestled in Styrofoam, wrapped in plastic. I know how to make arroz con pollo, even pernil for special occasions. But my mother never taught me how to wrestle a chicken that is whole, and she's been dead for six months.

I could call my tías, but I don't want them to feel sorry for me, sorry for not keeping in touch. They left the island and scattered like rain across the East Coast. Florida, New Jersey, New York, Pennsylvania. It feels insurmountable, synchronizing our disparate lives, dissecting and practicing the meaning of *closeness*. We're too busy sopping up rivers with washcloths.

So, I scrape my memories to see what comes up.

The bones we pulled from meat held between our teeth and discarded. The spoon my mother used for stirring and scooping and raising in warning. Her soft body leaning over the counter, an occasional glance at the pot to keep it from boiling over. Her voice when it did, the graceful rise and dip of her fury.

But I can't recall watching her handle a whole chicken, finding the right places to cut. I only remember her memories, like the one where she's plucking feathers as a child, chicken bodies held between her skinny knees.

The internet offers culinary advice and more.

There are 1,947 Latinos living here in Stillwater, 84 Puerto Ricans, not including me. I try to imagine how they look, but they're obscured by the red dust of Oklahoma wind and soil. I wonder what circumstances brought them to this cowboy town devoid of bodegas. How I might find them. How they might receive me.

I watch a nauseating instructional video, a close-up of a white woman's pink fingers gripping pinker flesh.

Three years ago, I fell in love with a white man and his gentle handling. He approached carefully while I puffed and strutted, then showed me ways of passion that didn't involve the screaming and slammed doors of my childhood. We moved west in pursuit of higher degrees, cheaper rent.

At first, we shared youthful cynicism—seeing death, for instance, as an overdue apology for life. In my romantic stupor, I failed to consider death beyond my own, how my mother's sudden departure would split me into *befores* and *afters*.

I pull out my knives, their cheap plastic handles and dull edges. They won't be enough, and I know, staring down at this raw body, its dense network of sinew and gristle, neither will I. The process would be too messy.

Despairing over poultry, I realize my problem is more than memory gaps and muscle. I review the certainties I have, the certainties I can work with.

What do I know?

One night six months ago, my mother wiped down the kitchen counters, prepared for bed, closed her eyes, and died.

I could get away with deceiving anyone who tries to sniff a region out of me, anyone who asks what I am, because I seem like something other than white, maybe.

Or I could drive an hour to the nearest Latin American grocery store, take note when the cashier looks me in the face and greets me in Spanish.

***

I could stop trying to make sense of myself.

What I couldn't do was prepare for her death, call her in advance for an exit interview. *How do you work through bones, Ma? How do you make a clean break?* She was a precious archive gone up in flames. But now, if given the chance to ask her just one question, it wouldn't be a question at all.

The chicken is back in my fridge, lying belly up and waiting for me to find the right tool to cut through its form. To separate the most tender pieces from its body.

I'm trying, Ma.

Unusable Tarot Reading from the Passenger Seat of a Crashed Peugeot 205 (1997)

Fee Griffin

So, my friend kisses a horse on the horse's face, breaks it gently to me that my car is haunted, cuts the deck. We drive to the seaside. Around us, puddles cough up spits of oil, slips of clay, root stock, rock salt, this sky rains *the business*. This guy will get out of his car, she predicts, like early morning children's TV, give up memories of a pond he can't place, of car chases and crows. There'll be a grease-green 90s toaster smashed and abandoned at an angle in a skip, elements like limbs in a reclined seat. There'll be a parting in the loosened area of reeds around the windshield, and we'll find ourselves outstretched on the tarmac, if not with the impact then with madness at how the sea can take a place over, behind and around your attention, grind the sharpness from glass, the ink from your eye. The nightless wonder of the unorbited, the outbid. Tassels from denim. Plastic from sand. Lean on the wing mirror with me a minute, OK? Did I tell you how big the sea has got?

Resurrecting
Maggie Yang

Grandmother shows me the different ways to crack
a walnut open. A snail surrendering
its shell, flattening into the pavement.

                                      Unpredictability becomes a sanctuary
                                      in my hands, the intimate folds stretching
                                      into light, draping me in the mist.

Evanescent, as I forget
what I was searching for. The kernel
tumbles out.

                                      The shells mountain on the kitchen table, the table
                                      lopsided as the surface renounces its name.
                                      My nails engrave into the ridges

only to remain shut—like everything else
in this room, decayed
in dichotomy.

                                      Grandmother's glasses sit on the ledge, her habits
                                      like prescriptions shoved in the back of a cabinet.
                                      The knife sits unbloodied, cutting board unripened

meat rotting in a takeout box
she didn't order. She refuses
to turn on the lights, convinced

                                        she can see through the walls. Because light
                                      fashions into words that deceive her. Dust
                                      is her companion, another tablecloth.

The hardwood floors become

a graveyard for sunflower seeds, multiplying
as they trickle from the bowl.

                                  The hinges to her bedroom door have given in to
                                  rust, curtains moth sanctified, light chased out
                                  through different cracks. Only her fingers

have not thinned, routine sculpted into calluses
counting the years like the rings of a tree stump.
She wonders why

                                  I have stopped painting scenes
                                  from her window, of her and grandfather,
                                  their faces melding into plasticized shipwrecks

of the west—a cityscape of elegies
kneeling and begging for me to unlearn

                                  the present.

After a Burial
Michael Beard

I pulled him out of the ground by his hair.
He had grown suddenly, deep
and unfurled in the bed of marigolds.
I sprayed his body clean with a garden hose,
light shower, the water clinging to every bare part of him.

I brought him inside, away from the reach of August heat,
found old clothes that needed another body to hold onto.
I offered breakfast, smoked ham and a mass of grits.
Nothing. He only wanted to eat handfuls
of marigold seeds. I watched his skin turn
bright orange after.

Five days now, and the walls of his chest
emit a glow, small room of light, clouds in his eyes.
To love someone is to keep them living.

We sleep in the same bed, eat all our meals together.
He doesn't speak, only sits
at the kitchen table during the day, echoed star.
Sometimes, he follows me out to the garden
just to sink his hands in the warm
dirt for hours, breathing marigold, a way to give in.

Augustine
Calgary Martin

The wind is blowing, and the hostas shift back and forth in the yard
like a cow's dumb head, like a cow's dumb, heavy teat, and the baby
inside me is dead. For days, we'd called it a fetus but learned when staring
into the dark tunnels of my radioscopic uterus it was still
an embryo, three weeks less mature than the calendar would suggest.
There is something melancholy in the air, like the sound of my living son
with his head tilted to the sky, calling out with the wind chimes,
Mooooommeeeeeeee. He sounds so far away. Earlier, having adapted so quickly
to what unfolded in a week—a crime scene on the bathroom floor, in the bowl
of the toilet, on the sheets where the towel folded up underneath me—
he runs in while I'm peeing, at last, without incident. The worst is over.
Yet, he has grown accustomed to it, and he is so young and accepts
so much that he shouldn't have to. As the wheels of his toddler legs grind
to a halt, he declares, *I wanna see some blood!* And he doesn't understand
the blood is finally gone, nor does he understand what left along with it.
Born on the shortest day of the year, he gives so much with his little
life. He is everything: the dark day we give thanks for at the end
of so many obscure months, the promise of the sun returning.

Wolf
Jesse Lee Kercheval

"When I was a girl,"
my mother told me as she was dying,
"a wolf always followed me
to my grandmother's house.

To protect me."

She was dying from too many cigarettes.
She was dying from too much Bourbon.

"That's Little Red Riding Hood, Mom," I said to her,
"and the Wolf is the villain."

"GOD DAMNIT," SHE SAID.

"THIS IS MY LIFE
NOT A FAIRY TALE.
THAT WOLF WAS THERE TO PROTECT ME,

FROM WILD BOARS

FROM BAD MEN,

FROM BAD MEN
LIKE MY FATHER,

FROM BAD WOMEN

LIKE MY GRANDMOTHER,
WHO WAS JUST LIKE HIM.

MY FATHER'S PRIZE POSSESSION
WAS A BULL.

"I THINK HE KNEW IF SOMETHING BAD HAPPENED TO ME,"
SHE SAID, "THE WOLF WOULD DO
SOMETHING JUST AS BAD TO THAT BULL.

When I was at my grandmother's house, I drew pictures of a wolf big enough to tear out her heart.

If she'd had a heart.

I KNEW THE WOLF WOULD DO EVERYTHING
IT COULD TO PROTECT ME.

But when I got appendicitis, my grandmother locked me in her house. She wouldn't let anyone call the doctor.

It was the wolf who broke down the door and saved me."

"You always said it was your mother."

"Yes," she said,

"It was my mother

PROTECTING ME.
AND ALL YOUR LIFE,

I'VE TRIED TO DO THE SAME."

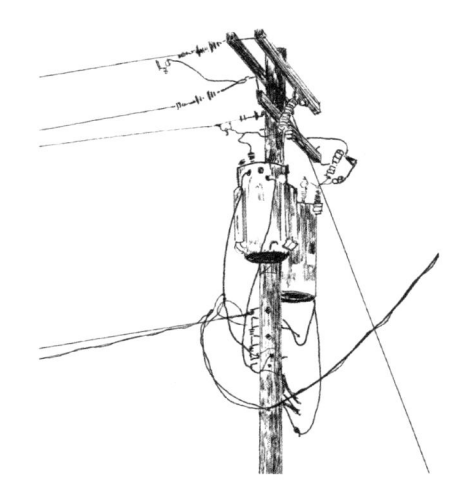

The Delivery Boy

RACHEL SALGUERO KOWALSKY

—

fiction

I. IN WHICH EVERYBODY FEELS CONFUSED
"Whatever might be is simply not there:
only murmurs, ripples, in the dark, in the night."
- Popul Vuh

De Los Santos Marcos, a Delivery Boy
Tuesday, 3 p.m.
De Los Santos looked up to gauge the position of the sun, but the sun was not there. Instead, above the sickly white tree that stood at the

edge of the garden, and above the many rooftops and sharp edges of the Brooklyn skyline, there was a gaping hole in the sky. Crouching inside the void was a feathered creature with the ruthless eyes of an owl and the thin, sharp teeth of a cat. A cold sweat gathered at his temples.

"Qué pasó, hombre?" asked Jerónimo, but De Los Santos could only point mutely at the sky.

Jerónimo followed his gaze. "Clouds? Pigeons?" They spoke Spanish, one man Guatemalan, the other Colombian.

De Los Santos shook his head. "A messenger," he said, saliva pooling in his mouth. He threw up his breakfast, spewing cornflakes and bile onto the dying grass.

Jerónimo put out his cigarette against the dusty earth, matter of fact, in the tight jeans and white T-shirt he wore to wait tables at Maya Café. "Don't be such a girl," he said. But now he was taking care not to look up. "Let's go back inside."

De Los Santos shook his head. The sharp teeth, the owl's eyes—they signaled death. His blood went cold. "My mother!"

"What about her?" Jerónimo was already headed across the garden to the safety of the café.

"I have to go."

Jerónimo turned back, his broad face serious. "You can't, you'll be fired." He gestured beyond the garden's gate. "Where will you go?"

"To find Maximón."

"Who the devil is Maximón?"

"A god," he began. But that wasn't right. "An idol." De Los Santos spoke more Kaqchikel than Spanish, which already lacked important words. "He's made of wood. You bring him rum, cigarettes…And he helps." He pushed through the gate.

Jerónimo shook his head. "I don't know your Guatemalan witchcraft."

It wasn't witchcraft, he thought, fumbling with his bicycle lock. Maximón provided relief and counsel, necessary as breath. De Los Santos had brought a cheap figurine on his crossing and placed it lovingly on the only table in his cousin's apartment in Bensonhurst, beneath a poster of Britney Spears. It had been a great comfort to him during these first nine weeks in the United States, but it was only a figurine. He needed the real thing, the life-sized Maximón in his black suit and hat. Back in San Lucas, Maximón reposed in a room of flowers, candles, and incense. He also resided in Santiago, San Andres, Xela, and, De Los Santos hoped, New York.

The lock fell open; his bicycle was free. De Los Santos hopped on board.

Cars whizzed by. Disembodied sounds reached his ears: a woman laughing, reggaetón, the carnival blare of an ice cream truck. Panic buzzed in both ears.

***

Gary, the Resident in Charge of Area A
Tuesday, 6 p.m.
"Shit, somebody just registered," said Gary. Then, "Wait, shit, the registrar fucked up the name."

Alta Gracia, the intern, peered at her screen. "Marcos, De Los Santos," she read aloud. "Bicycle accident."

"That's not a name," said Gary. Registration was constantly fucking up names, switching out vowels, and dropping hyphens. It slowed him down because nobody could place orders until the patient's name was correct in the system, and was that too much to ask?

"Maybe it is a name," said Alta Gracia, constantly aggrieved by the state of the world. "His name. De Los Santos."

"I'm gonna go ahead and guess his real name is Marcos," said Gary. He was the senior resident in charge here.

Alta Gracia blinked her enormous eyes. "Perhaps we should ask him," she said, and she blinked slowly, spoke slowly, it was torture.

The icon indicating Spanish-fucking-speaker popped up. Gary paused, considered. Alta Gracia spoke Spanish, but she was egregiously slow, a living nightmare in this emergency room. All day, every day this week. He turned to the medical student instead. "He's yours."

"Mine?" Brittany Brathwaite looked up from her textbook. She was skinny and severe, her hair pulled back in a knot.

"You're from Guam, right? You speak Spanish?"

She inclined her head, not gracing him with a response. She carried herself that way, he thought, like she disapproved of him. Yet he liked her. She was smart and driven, didn't leave halfway through her shift to take her fucking yearbook photo, and never abandoned her patients to "just grab some lunch." She was a soldier, the real deal.

Now another patient popped up on the board: a five-year-old girl with seizure x 3; at the same time, his phone vibrated—Mom. He silenced it.

The charge nurse stuck her head in the room. "Gary. The girl who seized looks bad. Also, you have two kids to sew, one with fever, and a Spanish kid who fell off his bicycle." She smiled sadly at him, half angel, half boss, she who saved his ass and handed it back to him daily. "Have you eaten?"

His phone vibrated again. Gary shook his head. Fuck that. He needed to get control of this fucking ER.

***

Alta Gracia, the Mexican Intern Who Had Been Educated in the United States
Tuesday, 6:10 p.m.

Acetaminophen had many names—Tylenol was just one of them. It was also called paracetamol, Panadol, Mapap, etc. In order to prevent double-dosing, she always asked families whether any of these were already given. She asked several different ways because some didn't consider acetaminophen a medicine, at least not in the same way as, say, albuterol or insulin.

"Hey Alta, did you put in my Tylenol order?" Iris, the charge nurse, was asking.

"Sorry—I need to pop into the room first. Which is it?"

"Room five, the kid with a fever. Pérez."

"Oh." Doom settled over her shoulders. Pérez would be Spanish speaking, which meant she'd be sucked into the room and held indefinitely, unable to leave as the clock hands churned mercilessly through the minutes. The moment she came through the door—brown, big-eyed, and familiar—the Latinxs told her everything. They asked every question they'd saved up over years of visits to English-only doctors, like, "Why does my son breathe fast after eating mangos?" They pressed iPhones into her hand to video chat with tío or tía or abuelita back home and explain that yes, Flaco had broken his leg, but no, he would not need surgery, gracias a Dios. There was no such thing as "popping into room five" if it contained the Pérez family and you were Alta Gracia Tierrafuego de la Paz. There was only a journey, an odyssey, a comingling of fates. She was ashamed of this, her disinclination to engage, but the currency of the ER was speed.

"Alta?" said Iris. "Please. He's burning up."

"Sorry." She clicked open the chart. A four-year-old, 13 kilos. Could that be right? It seemed small for a four-year-old.

Now Brittany and Gary were back in the workroom, possessed by la rabia of the ER, that strange, pressured frenzy that overtook every doctor and nurse in its yellow corridors and artificial light.

"Iris, I need a line and labs for the seizure girl," said Gary.

"I need a Tylenol order," the nurse retorted.

"I need to discuss the boy with the bicycle accident," said Brittany.

"Nobody's stopping you," said Gary. He was such a jerk. While he spoke, his fingers flew over the keyboard, and the Tylenol order was in.

Brittany Brathwaite began to speak. She had a British accent with, Alta Gracia thought, a hint of island in it. "De Los Santos Marcos is a seventeen-year-old Guatemalan male who reports that he saw a messenger—or a demon—then got on his bicycle in search of a large idol to help save his mother and was struck by the opening door of a taxi."

Alta Gracia sat up.

Gary's face went tight. "I'm sorry, what?"

"It is his chief complaint," Brittany said in a serious voice. "Saw a demon, struck by taxi." Alta Gracia really took her in then: her straight back and intense eyes, the shiny clipboard she held in her hands. She wore a severe white blouse buttoned high up her neck, and the flatness of her chest beneath the stiff material made Alta Gracia awkwardly aware of her own enormous bosom.

Gary folded his arms and put his head down on the desk. "Just start from the beginning."

"The patient reports that he was in the garden of the restaurant where he works as a delivery boy when he looked up and saw this demon. Because it resembled an owl and a cat, he understood it as an omen of his mother's imminent death. To preempt this, he rode his bicycle into Manhattan looking for some kind of doll..." She looked down at her notes.

"Can we skip this part?" Gary said from somewhere between his folded arms. "Can we talk about the door that smacked him in the head?"

Brittany nodded primly. "He was struck by the door of a taxi as it opened on 49th Street and fell to the ground. No loss of consciousness or vomiting. On further questioning, he is allergic to a red plant that comes out in February—"

"I'm gonna stop you right there," said Gary, tousled head raised like a plumed serpent. The room grew tense, the air suddenly thin. "Does. He. Have. A. Headache?"

"I am sorry. I forgot to ask."

"Go back in," said Gary. "We need to know. It is the whole fuc— the whole point of the interview. To find out what his symptoms are right now."

***

Back at Yale, Alta Gracia had majored in Latin American history and written her senior thesis on the Popul Vuh. She had been thinking, during these frenetic weeks, that she would like to write an ethnography of the emergency department, with its confluence of patients, students, residents, and specialists, each with their own modes of self-expression, their own individual and collective needs and wants. She would begin by comparing the ER to Tulan, the *Popul Vuh*'s Tower of Babylon, and end by pronouncing that, considering the vagaries of word choice, things omitted—or worse, assumed—and the fogginess of context and perspective, it was amazing that any patient's story survived at all.

Now Brittany was holding forth that she had no access to a translator. There was no phone in the room, and hers was out of battery.

Alta Gracia dove for her bag, extracting a charger. "Use this!"

Gary glowered. "I thought you spoke Spanish."

"No, Gary," said Brittany. "I am from Guyana—The only country in South America with English as its official language." After a moment, she added, "I speak English."

Gary pounded hard on his desk. "Who here speaks fucking Spanish?"

"I do," said Alta Gracia. He knew it perfectly well.

"Go see Mister Marcos Santos de los Marcos. Ask if he has a headache. And figure out the deal with the fucking demon."

"Okay."

"Alta!"

Two words. Her name was two words. High Grace. If you used only the first word, it was no longer her name. It was an adjective with no object, no purpose in life. She turned back from the door.

"Call a fucking psychiatrist."

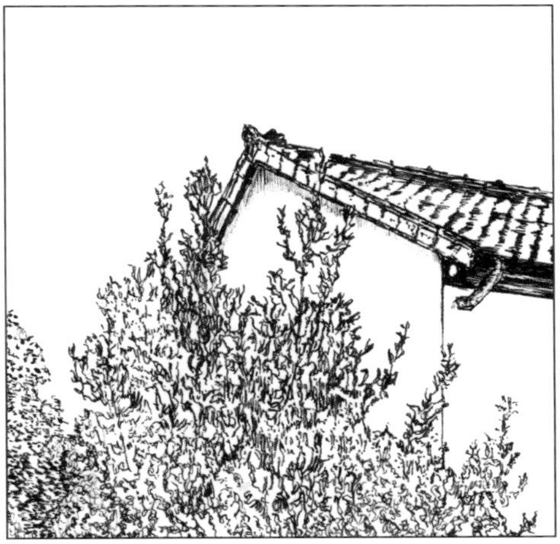

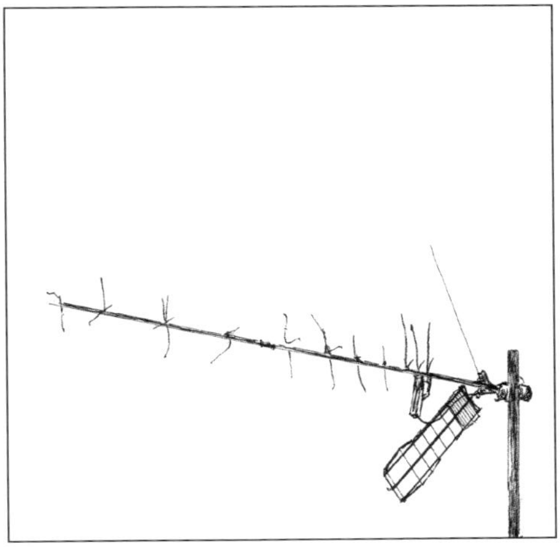

II. IN WHICH SEVERAL STORIES ARE TOLD, AND GARY GROWS ANGRY(ER)

"'Where did you come from? I don't know your faces.
What are your names?' said Earthquake."

- Popul Vuh

De Los Santos Marcos with a Psychiatrist Who Had Been to Honduras
Tuesday, 8:30 p.m.

Through the curtain, De Los Santos could see the little girl shaking. She shook as though possessed, a living cataclysm of tall buildings and blue lakes, tricksters, and fire. And then, because all human suffering is drawn from the same well, he turned to the messenger, whom the telephone translator had called "demon," and asked, "How will my mother die? And when?" But she only preened and pecked at the floor with her curved beak. Hot tears slid down his cheeks.

Alta Gracia had run from the room with the nurse named IRIS, but now another woman stepped inside, her shocking red hair sticking out like the spikes of a rambutan.

"I'm a doctor of the sentiments," she said in terrible Spanish. "Do you have intimate knowledge of this place?"

He did not trust himself to speak and only shook his head.

"I'm very sad there is no telephone for calling a translator," the redhead continued. "But I have been to Honduras."

Her smile was kind, and she wore green sneakers, which signaled new life, the gratification of sex, and wealth. A green candle lit before Maximón meant money would come soon. Her Spanish was poor, but his was not perfect either.

"Where are you during this minute? Do you know?"

"Consejo." He'd never been inside the hospital, but he knew it from the billboards around the city. It was called Our Lady of Good Counsel. The Americans, as was their custom, had moved letters around and removed the final O, but otherwise, they had left the word intact. The billboards were magnificent, like the poster of Britney Spears at Dino's restaurant and key shop; one could see in Britney's eyes her struggle to attain greatness, the inner light that guided her. Each billboard likewise showed careworn people whom one assumed had been gravely ill but had been guided back to life and health by the doctors, who walked these hallways, and by the power of the building itself, which was present in all the billboards, backlit like a religious image, shining with divine mystery and comfort. He understood it could only have been fate that brought him here when the taxi door had opened so shockingly into his face.

He had descended into Consejo as if through a tunnel, after the long, roaring ride through unknown streets—so many streets!—then rolled down a labyrinth of ramps and halls to arrive at this windowless place, the messenger atop the shoulder of the orderly. She was an incurious bird—he had expected her to fly about, exploring, but she stayed close.

They—he and the messenger—had been greeted by two nurses, like the manikins who greeted the twins in the underworld in *Popul Vuh*. He'd read it in primaria. Their nametags said, "IRIS SHE HER" and "NANCY SHE HER." They must have been sisters or cousins.

IRIS had fine black hair and slanting, dark eyes. She wore a pearl bracelet with a dangling sun and the word "*Manila*," her daughter or her city. "I need you to breathe," she said in Spanish, and he tried, although his breath did not come easily. He blamed this on his loneliness. How harshly his roots had been torn! They tore as he crossed into the US, when he arrived in New York, and as he climbed the stairs to his cousin's airless apartment at the end of each day. How it had cost him to learn the many streets of Brooklyn! And how his spirit ached when customers lifted the food from his hands and turned away to nourish their own families.

IRIS pressed a cold pack to the lump on his forehead and guided him to a room. The messenger fluttered in behind them, her yellow eyes darting from the sink to the shining rows of cupboards and the bed with its clean white sheets. The nurse pressed a colorful ball into his hand and pantomimed squeezing it hard.

The student doctor arrived next: Brittany Brathwaite. She was black as a Garifuna, which would have shocked him weeks ago, but now he knew many people in New York were black. The people were black, umber, yellow, and gray here; their hair was like cornsilk or the branches of trees, or like rope or fruit or the gnarled tail of a dog.

Alta Gracia came next, briefly, but ran off when the child began shaking. He wished she had not gone. Her intelligence made him shy. He, himself, had made it no further than the fifth grade. Her large eyes held a bit of condescension as she looked from his hair to his cheap shoes, but she spoke his language—his second language. His first was Kaqchikel.

His shoes had cost 250 quetzales, enough to take his sweetheart to Dino's for dinner, then to dance at El Condor and drink two beers—but in the United States, they were not considered good shoes. Jerónimo, from Café Maya, said they were not constructed properly.

Jerónimo was Colombian, a good man, but he had been in the United States a full year, and he didn't understand De Los Santos's position. For example, De Los Santos needed a new key for his bicycle lock. Jerónimo told him a key could be made at Jomdibo, and he wrote down an address that De Los Santos could not decipher. He would never find Jomdibo, nor, he reflected, would he ever find Maximón in this dizzying city.

Maximón! The wide, warm eyes that were always open; the heart that knew one's suffering!

"Marcos," the redhead said rather loudly. "Would you be interested in sitting down?"

He was surprised to find that he was still on his knees. He had been like that for some time…since Alta Gracia had exited. He stood and eased back towards the stretcher, keeping an eye on the messenger. She was preening now, her small, sharp teeth gleaming in the yellow light. Did the redhead see her? He thought not.

"I feel glad that you know your location. Do you know the date of this day?"

He squeezed the multi-colored ball. The messenger bared her teeth at him, and he threw it at her, missed. The redhead jumped. "It is the 20th of July," he said in Spanish.

She scribbled something on a notepad. "Where were you going this day on your bicycle?"

The bicycle! His cousin's, and now he'd lost it. "I was looking for the sun."

"I was told you were looking for…" She flipped through her notebook. "A doll."

"Maximón," he said.

"Mashimoan?" So strange coming from her, and now he saw that she had sky-blue eyes with life and movement to them, like water. "I'm sorry. I don't understand."

They sat in silence then, and the messenger flew down to rest on the redhead's shoulder. He thought of the blue lake under the glinting sun, the lap of the water against the dock, the trees that cast their shadows. The world was a deep bowl, and the lake filled it up. Sometimes the clouds hung low; he walked through them and breathed them in. He thought of the dogs, the snakes, the bats, the heavy moon. Even the owls were beautiful back home when the death they announced was another person's. Then it was just the cycle of life and death, two sides of a pebble.

"Wait!" she slapped her forehead, dug into the pocket of her white coat, and produced a phone. She held it up as though a butterfly had landed in her palm, and she was delighted by this turn of events, the tenacity of the butterfly, and the faith such a butterfly must have that it could land here and not be captured or crushed or devoured by the crepuscular bird with its awful teeth. She typed on her phone and waited. "Spanish, please."

A genial man introduced himself on speaker. "Please tell me, what brought you to the hospital?"

"A messenger came to warn me about my mother's death."

Hesitation on the line. "An actual messenger, or is this a figure of speech?"

"An actual messenger."

This was translated.

The bird let out a screech, shaking her feathers. Turquoise, red, yellow, silver—Impossible to ignore, but the redhead didn't react. Instead, she asked, through the translator, "Have you called your mother?"

"She doesn't answer."

"Her friends?"

"Dino doesn't answer either."

"Who?"

"Her boss—and mine before I came here. He has a restaurant and key shop. He also sells posters of celebrities, like Britney Spears."

The old man had taught him to work the key-cutting machine, starting with the placement of the tracer and blade and then the proper alignment of each key. He'd taught De Los Santos many things: how to clean the machine, repair it when broken, and also how to please his sweetheart in the cemetery behind the church…this in extremely specific terms he appreciated deeply, as his father had disappeared long before.

In New York, he had no sweetheart, no Dino, no mother. His cousin was barely home, he drank too much, and he befriended men who didn't care about him.

The redhead ran her hand through her strange, lovely hair. "De Los Santos, you look sad."

He hid his face in his hands.

She came toward him in her green shoes. "Hey, it's okay. A lot of people feel sad in New York City." The translator translated, his voice solemn and kind.

The redhead's brows were knit as though she were waiting for De Los Santos to speak but listening to another voice as well, perhaps of all the science that she knew, which was, of course, extensive. Her red hair was a beacon up above him, its own sort of brilliant sun. "You want to find Mashimoan because he is like… like a cure for you. He's a helper for you. Is that right?"

Maximón was Maximón. He didn't know the Spanish words or if they even existed. "Yes."

The translator sighed and addressed him directly. "Hombre, there is no Maximón in the United States. Well, maybe in California. Not here."

Now an angry doctor entered, eyes big as a rabbit's. His nametag said GARY. "IsHeCrazy?" GARY shouted. "Yesorno, yesorno, yesorno?"

* * *

Gary, the Resident in Charge of Area A
Tuesday, 10:40 p.m.
"Gary. What the hell?" His mom was an angry blond woman, usually on skis. They were not close.

"I'm working."

"Do me a favor."

The psychiatrist he'd dragged from the delivery boy's room stood beside him, smiling like a Hare Krishna.

"I bought ski pants, but they auto-populated to your address instead of mine. Can you overnight them? UPS does it. They're twenty-four hours."

Iris appeared. "Gary, your endotracheal tube is in the right mainstem. For the little girl with the seizure."

"Just buy them again. With your address."

"What?" Iris arched her brows and played with her bracelet.

She was his only friend here. No, fuck that, she hated him. She just played nice to keep the ER moving. He'd intubated the seizure kid on the first try, hot shit, but the bad news was he had mainstemmed it: he was only ventilating one fucking lung. "Not you. Thank you. My mom."

"I need them this weekend."

"Buy different pants."

"Gary. The tube." Iris was getting upset.

Kowalsky 89

He couldn't hang up, but he couldn't stay on the phone either. He set it down grimly.

"Need a minute?" asked the redhead, the psychiatrist. She was way too smug.

"I need a diagnosis for this Guatemalan."

"Is there anyone who knows his baseline mental status?" she asked. "We can't reach his mother."

"What's the point? She won't speak any English."

"Or Spanish," pointed out Alta, aggrieved, as usual, that he hadn't read the fucking memo about indigenous people or languages.

***

Everybody stood in the workroom and discussed the delivery boy. The psychiatrist thought he might have susto, which she'd learned about during her extensive two-week experience in Honduras, and described it as "a Spanish way of being scared." Brittany suggested opiate withdrawal; perhaps he had used Blue Demon, a street drug, but Gary nixed that one. His mom blew through Percocet like fucking Tic Tacs; he knew it when he saw it.

His phone vibrated so violently that it nearly leaped off the counter. Mom. He ignored it and rose heavily to his feet. He was tired and fucking hungry. He followed Iris out of the room like a schoolboy. At the threshold, he turned and pointed at Alta Gracia. "Scan his head."

"I am not comfortable with that plan."

"Just do it."

"I need a diagnosis." She was stalling. "I can't put the order in the computer without a diagnosis."

"Susto," he said, spotting a mother lode of graham crackers at the nurses' station.

"If you already know, why expose him to radiation?"

"It's a diagnosis of exclusion. He could be having a stroke. We don't know. We don't know anything about anyone. Only what they tell us."

He snagged some grahams, ripped the packaging, and crammed two into his mouth.

"It is inequitable to expose him to radiation just because we cannot understand him."

Gary laughed. She was so self-righteous, so principled, the luxury of those who aren't yet responsible for anything. "What if he went home and died, and his paperwork said *susto*? Bye, bye, medical license. Hello, lawsuit. Hello, front page of the *New York Times*: medical doctors stereotype Hispanic patient who then goes home and dies."

He could see the anger in her black eyes. She knows I'm right, he thought. She's angry, but she knows I'm right.

***

Alta Gracia, the Mexican Intern Who Had Been Educated in the United States
Tuesday, 8:30 p.m.
The trouble with English speakers was that they always made you wait for the noun. The girl was having an unprovoked first-time afebrile seizure. But by the time Iris got to "seizure," precious moments had gone by, and Alta Gracia had ridden a roller coaster of uncertainty from dog bite to migraine to asthma attack. Unmoored with no noun, she had forgotten what she hoped for in this world, let alone the sentence. This was how they wore you down.

"Let's go!" said Iris. "Fast!"

She hesitated. Safe, correct, fast—that was her hierarchy of intention. Fast was for bandits and birds of prey.

***

When she'd first entered the delivery boy's room, the psychiatrist hadn't arrived, so it was just herself and De Los Santos Marcos. She'd meant to bring ice cream to room five on her way, but Bonifacio WhatsApp'd her. Faced with competing urgencies—her boyfriend, room five, the delivery boy, and a sudden, oppressive hunger, she'd chosen to do her work.

"I'm Dr. Tierrafuego de la Paz. Please call me Alta Gracia. I'm from Yucatán, Mexico, and I've brought you ice cream."

"That's very good," he said.

The boy on the bed was awkward, out of context, fidgeting with the stress ball they gave teenagers at triage. His eyes darted around the room, from countertop to ceiling to floor, as though following an insect's flight. They were dark and serious, close-set. His upper lip was the cupid's bow of a movie star, a bird in flight. He reached for the ice cream.

She handed him a plastic spoon from the breast pocket of her coat. He wiped it carefully on the sheet, pulled up the top of the single-serve container, and peered inside with interest.

She tore open another package, fished out a spoon, and fell to eating.

Her patient wore the uniform of New York City delivery boys: worn jeans (clean but faded), a t-shirt, and cheap sneakers. His thick hair stood straight up and had dust in it, or maybe lice. Where, she wondered, were the Latinx prep-school boys, the lacrosse players, the heirs of rum and sugar? They had pediatricians and bicycle helmets.

"De Los Santos, do you remember how you got here?"

"Oye," he said, looking up from his untouched ice cream. It was an invitation to listen, a turn of phrase she loved in her grandmother's mouth, but not in this mad place. "Do you know San Lucas Tolimán?" he asked.

"No, I'm sorry. But do you remember colliding with a taxi?"

"It is my town." He glanced up above the supply cabinet, then back at her. "Well, there was a mudslide in Santa Clara. My uncle died, and my aunt and cousins came to live with us. Aricely, Gladys, Heidy, y La Gorda. You can imagine we needed money."

"But that was not today."

"No," he agreed.

She glanced up at the clock. The boy chucked the ball hard at the far wall of the room. It bounced off and struck the trash can.

"De Los Santos, I have been told you see a demon. Is that true?"

"A messenger." He pointed into the corner.

"There?"

He nodded.

She stepped around the stretcher. "I don't see anything. No demon, no messenger."

"Bien," he said—rendible either as "good" or "yes, you do."

She opened another ice cream. "What is the message?"

"Te voy a contar una historia," he said—I'm going to tell you a story. No, a history. A lengthy tale with roots and context. Such a thing could never live or breathe here.

Her phone buzzed—Bonifacio. She stepped out.

**

"Boni, I can't talk."

"You are talking now."

They had met over the summer, both city kids visiting their grandparents in the country. When Bonifacio showed up at the door with a bouquet of monjas blancas, Abuelita had ushered him into the salon off the courtyard, handed him a cold Tecate, and pulled up a chair. They spoke—the three of them—of school, horticulture (his parents were professors), Lorca, and Nicky Jam. One night the lights went out, and the dark settled over them. The scent of the orange trees in the courtyard, the dimness of the room, the yellow velvet chairs, the cry of the birds above.…The creak and settle of the old Spanish house. When Abuelita had gone for a flashlight, he reached for her hand in the dark. Just that. And then he had whispered in her ear.

Bonifacio's sexual powers ran the length of his oratory apparatus, starting at Broca's area and ending with his soft, urgent voice. Sometimes she would reach for him, wrap her hands in his fine black hair, and find herself uncharacteristically unable to think a single thought. His verbal abundance canceled her out entirely, stilled, and stunned her.

"When is your vacation?"

"We don't have vacation."

"Of course you do."

How could she tell him there was no time for vacation (from the Latin vacāre—to be free, to have respite) in this speed-crazed life?

"Mi amor," came Bonifacio's softening voice, "no aguanto"—I cannot bear this separation. But he would have to. They both would.

"I'll call you after," she said. She touched her fingertip to the red telephone icon, and Bonifacio was gone.

***

Back in the room, the delivery boy was throwing out his ice cream. He did so gently, like a mover loading fragile cargo. "It is too cold," he explained. He laid the spoon on the counter.

"Let us focus," she said. "You see a messenger."

"My mother always cared for us," he said. "Myself, my brothers, and sisters. You know, there are gangs in our towns. The boys go bad, but my mother didn't permit this. Instead, she taught us that Maximón provides. I had to find him."

"When?"

"When I looked up. For the sun."

The ice cream soured in her stomach. His story was like *Popul Vuh*, chronologically impaired, full of time warps and dead ends. The ancient text began with creation, jumped to an intrepid set of hero-twins, then backtracked to their father and uncle, barely remembering to finish up the world it had so painstakingly begun.

Mayan narrative was associative, not chronological—her Latin American lit prof's favorite talking point. Back then, studying for her final, she'd tried to summarize *Popul Vuh,* fixing the result to her dormroom wall with double-sided tape.

PREAMBLE:

Two gods: Xpiyacoc, Xmucane.

BOOK ONE:

Sea and sky, three more gods, land.
Plumed sea serpent makes animals.
Gods make humans: first from mud, then wood.
Wooden people become monkeys.
A large bird pretends to be the sun.

* * *

It was meaningless. The night before the final, stomach ravaged by nervios and Diet Coke, she'd realized her error. She took a fresh piece of paper and wrote:

When will the sun rise?
What is a human being?

* * *

She'd earned an A+, but it had not been easy, and here she was again, trying to crack the code.

How to get to the heart of the story? They were not so different, she and this delivery boy—they both spoke Spanish and were moved and motivated by love. They were tangential thinkers, ambos, distracted by the butterfly at the edge of the machine. Yet he was as foreign, as unknowable to her, as Brittany Brathwaite, with her punctiliousness and British accent.

Could one person ever truly know another? The answer was no, ¡que no! Had De Los Santos Marcos been her identical twin and suckled at her own mother's breast, he would still and always be a mystery because he lived outside her skin, like everyone else on the planet.

But, surely, one had to try.

A buzz of her phone, Bonifacio. Then Iris's dramatic entrance: "The five-year-old with the unprovoked first-time afebrile seizure—she's in status epilepticus. Gary needs you."

Alta Gracia turned to the delivery boy—he was rising to his feet, taking in the sudden commotion. "Please," she said. "Tell me! Do you have a headache? Right now?" There were tears in his eyes. He was miserable. She lowered her voice, pleading with him, urgent as a lover. "Yes or no?"

"Let's go!" said Iris. "Fast!"

She hesitated, contemplating her hierarchy of intention: safe, correct, fast.

The delivery boy fell to his knees.

She raced past him as the psychiatrist entered, calling apologies over her shoulder. And then she was at the child's side.

But not right away. Before she entered the room, before she inserted a second large-bore IV—seeing the flash of blood at its stem, pushing saline through it for all she was worth, and showing Gary, Iris, and all the world that this Mexican girl knew her shit—she read Bonifacio's text. "I am thinking of your body," it read. Then (noun first): "Tu cuerpo: lindo, generoso, iluminado, adorado, y deseado"— beautiful, generous, moonlit, adored, and desired (by me).

III. IN WHICH MOST PEOPLE FEEL BETTER

"It all came together as they went on thinking in the darkness, in the night, as they searched and they sifted, they thought, and they wondered."

- Popul Vuh

De Los Santos Marcos, a Delivery Boy
Tuesday, 10:30 p.m.

De Los Santos was alone with his fear. Everyone was gone: Iris, Brittany, Alta Gracia, the redheaded sentiment doctor, and Gary. The messenger perched next to him, eerily still in the ER's perpetual light. Perhaps she *was* a demon, conjured by an evil eye. He squeezed his own eyes shut, and she smiled at him from under his lids. Her face was a maze of tattoos, like the boys in the gangs, her eyes made of his own thin vessels, alive with the light and electricity of his body. Now she pressed herself against him, the feel of dry kindling against his skin, until their pulse became one and the same. She fluttered her dark wings against his heart.

Thoughts of his mother crowded his mind like people in a subway car or spoons and forks in the amazement of a dishwasher. Her reassuring skin. Her bright huipiles, which grew soft over time, the thick rope of her hair.

He fell into a fitful sleep, the messenger curled up on his chest.

* * *

"We are going to get a kyat-scan of your brain," Brittany said in English, and the translator said, "Kat-escong." After some wandering down the hallway, poking her head into this room and that, the student had taken him to a telephone at the nurses' station. "Your thoughts are a bit disorganized," she said through the translator. "We are worried that your brain was injured when the taxi door struck you."

He did not feel disorganized, only sleepy, but he didn't disagree. "Of course you know best, and if that is what you think we should do, then naturally, we'll do it," he said. This was translated. Then he added, "I trust you." They were on speaker, and the words were quite loud. "ITRUSTYOU." People turned to look.

"There is a risk of getting cancer from the radiation," she continued. De Los Santos did not know what radiation was, but he understood cancer to be a very grave condition. He had known a man with cancer on his nose that consumed his face and neck. A little cousin had grown yellow and shriveled up and died; later, people said she had cancer. But it didn't seem that something in this place of northern science could give him cancer. He discounted the idea.

The kat-escong was a beautiful machine, a perfect round *O* with a thin, silver tongue emerging from its depths, and on the tongue, they lay him down beneath a white blanket. "Don't move," said the technologist in Spanish and left the room. He was alone.

The machine drew him into its iron heart.

* * *

As the orderly wheeled him back into the room, his phone rang. He flipped it open.

"Wal!" – my son. It was his mother.

"I thought you were dead," he said, shaking. "I saw a messenger."

"Your messenger brought you news of Dino Abaj. He is dead, not me."

"How?"

"It was his heart." She was crying.

De Los Santos closed his eyes. He would miss the old man but was ashamed to find that, primarily, he was happy. His mother was alive.

Now Alta Gracia stepped into the room with Gary. She lowered herself into a chair. "De Los Santos," she said in Spanish. "Your kat-escong is normal. It means your brain is okay, but Gary is still worried. He wants you to have more tests."

"The truth is," said De Los Santos, "My mother is well, and I'm not worried anymore. I'd like to go home now."

Alta Gracia's jaw went slack. "Just like that?"

"Well, why not?"

"You came to an emergency room! You took up our time!" She closed her eyes tightly, and when she opened them, they were full of dread. "Gary will be angry."

98 **BOOTH**

"That is true," he said. "But everything has been completed here." These were the final words of *Popul Vuh*. He'd liked the book when he'd read it in primaria, and while this ending seemed artificial (no story was ever completed), he could see that at some point, one had to move on.

Alta Gracia turned several colors— ghostly white, pink, then crimson with, he realized, shame— like a person who comes to Dino's and explains they have given their key to a lover, and the lover is suddenly gone.

"WhatDidHeSay?" said Gary. "WhatDidHeSay?"

"He said…" she began, in English. "He said." Then she froze, squeezing her eyes shut. "He feels." She pursed her lips, crossed her arms, and grabbed her shoulders. "Much. Better!" Her body began to shake, her long black ponytail jumped and bounced, she threw her head back; De Los Santos feared she was convulsing. But then laughter shrieked past her lips, a force of nature. It was loud and green, tall as a mountain ringed with clouds.

He smiled. He didn't know what was funny, but he liked laughing with her.

Perched atop the cabinet, the messenger watched with big, grave eyes. Being from the más allá, she probably found them strange.

* * *

De Los Santos stood outside the hospital, wondering how to get back to Bensonhurst. It was early morning, the sun edging up between the buildings. His messenger was perched atop a bicycle rack.

"Still looking for Maximón?" Alta Gracia had just exited Consejo. She stood blinking and smiling in the morning sun.

"Yes," he said, "but not today. I need to go to work, and Jumdibo."

"Humdipot?" She echoed him and scratched her head. He handed her the paper with Jerónimo's illegible scrawl. "Oh, you mean Home Depot." She pulled out a pen and wrote the words with care. "It's far from here. Why do you want to go?"

He rummaged in his backpack and pulled out his broken key. The edges were too smooth. They couldn't grip the innards of the lock. "It doesn't function."

"Oh!" she said. "In that case, just go to a key shop. There is one across the street." She pointed to where it said "HARDWARE."

"That's good," he said, amazed at his luck. With Dino gone, the key felt even more important. It was connected to his past as well as to New York City: the strange new skyline, Maya Café, his home on 18th Avenue. A way forward and back. "Thank you."

But the girl had already turned away. Her phone rang, and she'd pressed it to her ear with a look so colored by desire, he could not even name it. There were things that could not be expressed in any language. The way a root, still dripping earth, could grieve its original place yet remain alive, maintain its stem and its leaves.

His bicycle rested against the rack where the messenger preened her splendid feathers. She had done her job, brought news of home, and even kept vigil with him overnight. As Alta Gracia turned away, and the sun took up its spot in the sky, she ducked, swooped, flashed her brilliant feathers—turquoise, red, yellow, silver— showed her terrible teeth, then flew off above the rushing avenue into the generous sky above Consejo, over the key shop, into the allure of the ineluctable, the primarily cruel but unpredictably and lavishly compassionate, infinitely shaking city.

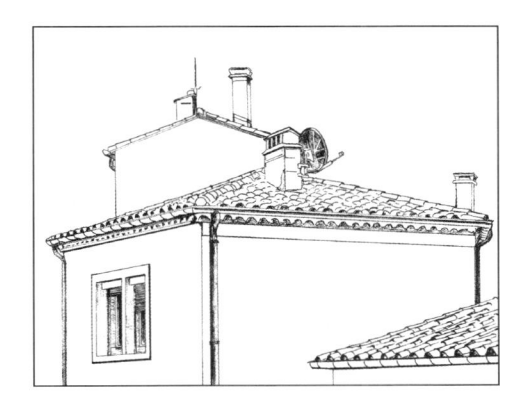

The Girl Goes Missing

COURTNEY CRAGGETT

—

fiction

THE GIRL GOES MISSING, AND HER FAMILY SOUNDS the alarm.

She has never been missing before—not like this, not for so long without warning. The girl is the light of the whole kingdom: radiant smile, golden laughter, lilac perfume. The king and queen never imagined this would happen.

The advisors say, "All girls wander at her age, even princesses." But, the king and queen know better, know that the girl is safe and loved and has no reason to leave on her own. Know that their story is different from every other story—or was supposed to be different—that in their story, the girl was never supposed to go missing at all.

They recount for the advisors the day they brought the girl home, small and pink, how she smiled weeks before she was expected to and laughed soon after. They are trying to say, "How could that joy become this sorrow?" It feels inconceivable.

What they do not know—or maybe know but do not realize—is that in every story, the girl goes missing. It's the way of the world.

The girl goes missing, and maybe she is in a tower with a sorceress who climbs her long hair.

And maybe she is in a cabin with seven dwarfs working in the mines.

And maybe she has pricked her finger and fallen asleep.

And maybe she is in a castle, teaching a beast to read.

In every story, the girl goes missing.

* * *

The king and queen throw themselves into finding her. They forget to sleep, to eat, sometimes even to breathe. Search parties chase every lead, investigators excavate everything that might be a clue, warriors threaten and interrogate. Someone must know something.

Their subjects write letters, letters that they must believe are a comfort. Letters that begin, "I understand. My girl went missing, too."

It's then the queen remembers when *she* went missing. She'd forgotten until now. She was twelve or thirteen, that age when so many girls disappear, and she can't remember how she was recovered.

The girl goes missing, and maybe she has lost her voice and now lives on land.

And maybe she has been turned into a swan by a wizard.

And maybe she is buried in the desert in Juarez.

And maybe she is discarded behind a dumpster.

And maybe she is hiding in her room with the curtains drawn dark. In every story, the girl goes missing.

***

In this story, after three days and three nights, the girl is found. The kingdom rejoices. Then the nightmares begin for the girl, for the king, for the queen. The celebrations play on by day, but at night, the king and queen comfort the girl, comfort each other. In every story, the girl goes missing, but after the story, *then* what happens? The king and queen post guards outside the girl's bedroom. They watch her every movement. They question and reason and try to understand. They wonder how they will ever move on.

Throughout the kingdom, parents write to ask what the girl did, what the parents did, how this could have all been avoided. They want a way out of this story. There is no way out of this story. This is the story.

The princess pours herself into her subjects. She reassures them that she is back now for good. She smiles at them with her radiant smile, laughs her golden laugh. Her subjects sigh in relief that all is well, but the queen hears the difference, understands that some part of her girl is gone forever.

***

Eventually, the girl grows up, and the kingdom forgets that she was ever missing. They are too preoccupied with their own daughters, the way they have begun to disappear, slowly, one by one. The girl too forgets, like her mother forgot, forgets until she has a little girl of her own: pink, squinty face, tiny baby grunts. Then, she remembers, and her dreams take her back to nightmares. Her daughter smiles and laughs and coos, and the girl cannot imagine a future in which she goes missing. She pours over the old stories, tries to find even one exception. The girl goes missing and she is lost forever, or she goes missing and she is found but a piece of her is missing, or she goes missing and she is found and then goes missing again. The girl's room fills with towers and towers of books. Every story the girl reads is the same. The girl goes missing. She cannot find another story.

It's then that the girl takes out a pen. She holds her sleeping baby against her chest, breath soft through parted lips, eyelashes fluttering. The girl holds her baby, and she holds a pen, and she begins to write.

In this story, the girl is here. She has always been here and always will be. In this story, she battles sorcerers and dragons and sea monsters but never disappears. In this story, even if the girl is cut down, she remains. In this story, when the journey is hard, there are more girls, all lined up in a row, refusing to fade away. The girl writes and writes until her arm is numb with writing. She writes her daughter a new story, and she will read the story aloud every night, like a prayer. And, one day, if her girl goes missing, and the advisors say that all girls go missing, and the kingdom writes letters that recount how in every story, the girl goes missing, the girl will stop them. She will hold up this story, its pages by then worn through by its nightly retelling, and she will say, No, not in every story, not this one.

A CONVERSATION WITH
Jo Ann Beard
SUSAN LERNER

interview

Many readers first encounter Jo Ann Beard through her essay "The Fourth State of Matter," published in The New Yorker *and included in the 1997 edition of* Best American Essays. *"The Fourth State of Matter" also appears in Beard's acclaimed collection* The Boys of My Youth, *which she followed with a novel,* In Zanesville. *In her recent collection,* Festival Days, *Beard's prose displays her signature precision as well as a refusal to acknowledge the gods of genre—true narratives incorporate fictional elements, and fiction stems from truth. Beard's writing is lauded for its laser-like attention to detail—every word, phrase, and sentence has been crafted with the precision of a diamond cutter. Her exquisitely honed images* *and ideas move her narratives forward organically, without a hint of artifice.*

The recipient of a Guggenheim Fellowship and Whiting Foundation Award, Beard teaches writing at Sarah Lawrence College. On December 1, 2022, Beard came to Indianapolis as a Butler Visiting Writer. During this time, she sat down with **Booth** *to discuss her feelings about prolific writers, ambition, and celebrity memoirs.*

Susan Lerner (SL): In terms of craft, I've always wanted to ask you about your use of the present tense. What draws you to it? What does it allow you to explore?

Jo Ann Beard (JAB): I'm never aware of things like tenses when I'm writing; that's just the way it comes out. It might have something to do with that idea of going deep inside and imagining it, like I'm watching the action as it's happening. So the present tense may reflect that immediacy of seeing the story unfold as I'm writing.

SL: It seems as though your thoughts and feelings and images come to you cinematically.

JAB: They do, like a daydream or something—but more deliberate than a daydream. In a memory piece, I like to think about what it really felt like to be in that place, what everything looked like and felt like.

SL: I'm curious as to how you remember the different things that made up that experience. How does that kind of sensory immersion happen for you? How do you help your students to do this?

JAB: Well, a lot of it is imagined as much as remembered. But over the years I've also discovered that you can train your memory. What you recall right at the beginning is not necessarily what you remember when you keep at it and keep trying. Though I think sometimes I merge memory with imagination.

SL: I would guess that maybe we all do that.

JAB: I think we all do that to some extent. I'm just doing it deliberately for the cause of the story or the essay. That said, I've given an assignment to my students that involves trying to teach them to sharpen their memory, having them just sit and make a list from memory of every single thing that's in their room: walk in the door, look to the right, what do you see. Write down everything you see. It works better for neatniks, obviously, but you'd be surprised what people can remember when they focus.

SL: In a *Bookforum* interview with Jenn Shapland, you said that you were lucky to have been rejected by the Iowa Writers' Workshop so early on, because it taught you about how *you* have to understand who you are as a writer and what your work is. I wonder how you answer those questions about yourself now.

JAB: Yes, the director of that program rejected me, and he did it in such a definitive way. He said, "Here's why we don't want you here," and then told me all the things about my writing that he said he literally couldn't bear to read. At the time, I thought that was really strange—and that he was wrong. First, he was wrong about my writing. Second, he was wrong as a teacher. There's nobody in the world you should say that to, and because I didn't want to quit writing, it forced me to ask, Is he right? Is he wrong? And if he's wrong, which I believed, then that means I know more about my work than he does. Therefore, I, in this situation, am the expert on what I'm doing, and he, Frank Conroy, knows less than I do. It was an important lesson, and that was the moment when part of me said to the other part of me: It is not good for you to be meek about your work, because if you are, you'll go away and you'll never come back again.

SL: For many other writers, that might have been the end, the crush. It's really remarkable.

JAB: It was crushing; it made me cry.

SL: But . . .

JAB: But, I thought, I know he's wrong; therefore, I know something about myself as a writer that even people who are supposed to know about writing don't know. It's served me well through all the rejection a writer has to experience. After graduating from my program, I had to get through years of people saying "no"—the way they do to everybody. Some people just can't bear it, and they'll go do something for which they hear "yes." There are many reasons why you would want to be that person. However, I wasn't.

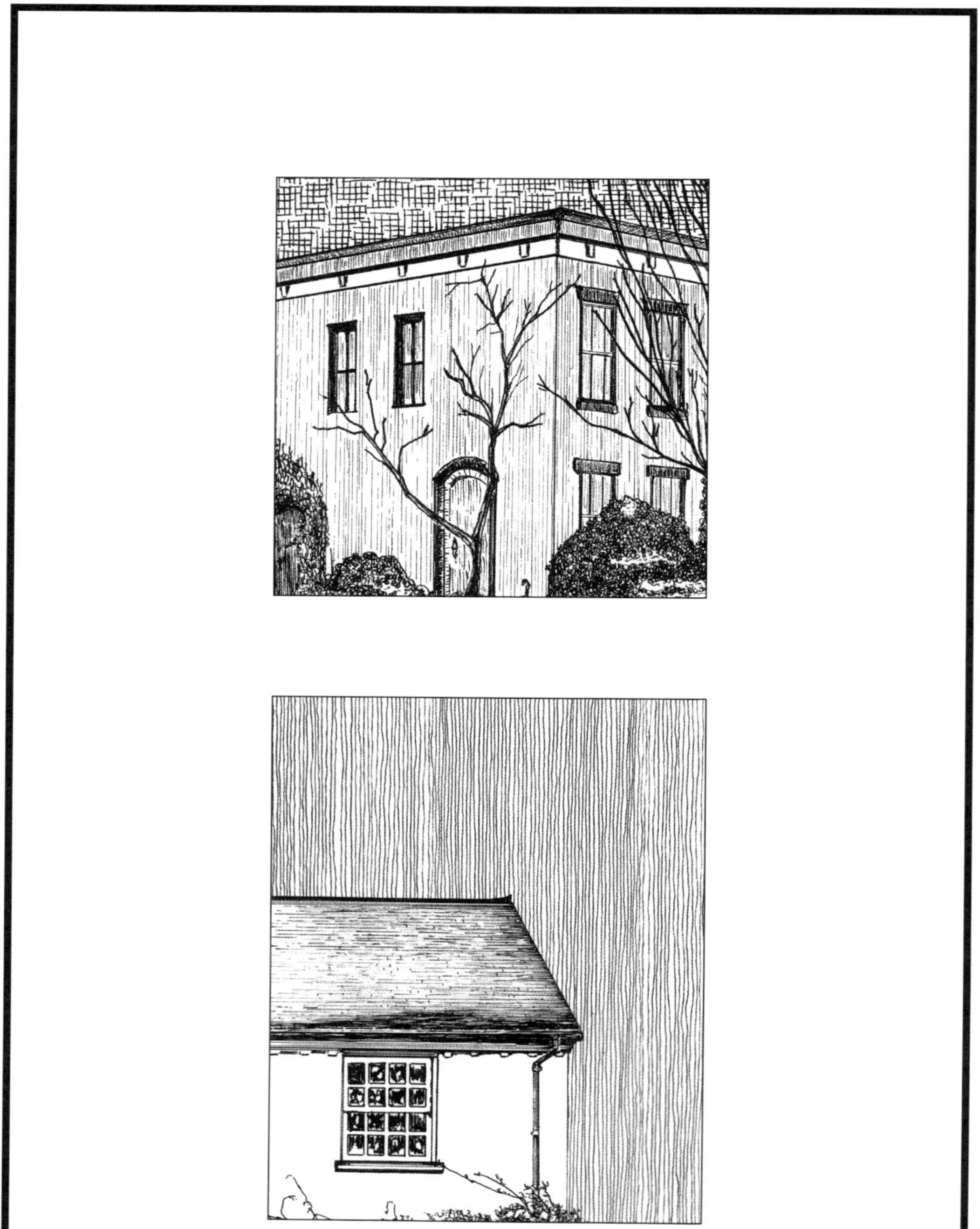

SL: I'm now thinking about how you describe the nature of your writing process. It strikes me as . . . uncomfortable?

JAB: Oh, it's awful.

SL: Okay, so, I wonder why you write. Perhaps the better question is, What keeps you writing?

JAB: In the past, what has kept me writing were the things that I wanted to write about. I would get interested in something, and want to explore it through writing. That's where all of my work has come from, just loving that discovery process.

SL: I think about how many of us are drawn to personal writing, and yet for many of us it simultaneously engenders reluctance and dread? Why do you think that is?

JAB: I can answer only for me, and for me it's because it's hard and I avoid difficult things. Our own stories are meaningless in light of the vastness of the world and of human experiences. So I have to figure out how to take this little slice of my life and force it to *mean* something, beyond myself. That is hard work.

SL: I have a question about "Werner" and about "Cheri." It's curious to me that you used real characters and the dramatic events that happened in their lives as a springboard from which to fictionalize. I wonder why you chose to do that rather than write those narratives in the form of literary journalism or, if you were to change enough of the material, simply as fictional short stories?

JAB: Somebody had offered to publish "Cheri" as fiction because they were uncomfortable with the imagined part of it. At first, I thought it did not make any difference how it's defined, but then it *did* make a difference to me—the fact that she was a real person who went Dr. Kevorkian, as opposed to a fictional character.

SL: It's interesting that it matters to you that that did happen to her.

JAB: This was a real person who had to say goodbye to her daughters and leave them deliberately and emphatically—she had made that decision to choose her moment. I was curious about that, what it felt like. I realized along the way that it felt like courage to me.

SL: I want to ask about John D'Agata, because you've just said that in "Cheri," the facts were important to you. In his writing, he's made it clear that the facts were not important to him. Can you talk about that?

JAB: I understand his impulse and his desire. He wants to imagine his way in and then create a story that's close or adjacent. To me, it's just important to be honest about what it is—even when it is something that resides in both camps, fiction and nonfiction. I didn't want "Cheri" to be called fiction, but I certainly didn't need it to be called nonfiction either. I think both of them are a little reductive and wrong, in terms of functioning as labels. And the labels are deceptive too—there isn't really anything that's fitting. Literary nonfiction doesn't exactly fit. Creative nonfiction is the same thing. Nonfiction definitely doesn't fit, and fiction definitely doesn't fit. So, what else is there?

SL: You don't think creative nonfiction encompasses the—

JAB: It seems like an all-purpose term, but, no, maybe none of it is exactly right, and I don't even care where my own work is concerned; it's hard enough to get it written. If I worked for a magazine or a newspaper, I would care a lot about what's fiction and what's nonfiction—even though I was not born yesterday and I know that even nonfiction isn't really nonfiction. Everything has a spin. I could take today's *The New York Times* front page and show you everywhere that our perceptions of these true stories are being shaped.

SL: Do you think there's something different about the nature of D'Agata's writing, that it more closely hews toward journalism and so it has an inherent responsibility to be factual, or do you think it's the same capacious kind of writing that you're doing?

JAB: I don't know, and I feel like I can't answer for another person. John is a little bit of a provocateur. If we can get somebody out there who is willing to provoke interest in "nonfiction writing," I'm all for it. We have enough provocateurs in every other field of interest. We have TikTok provocateurs, so why shouldn't John D'Agata be able to nudge the door open a little bit with nonfiction writing and let in a little air and see what happens?

SL: Would you write another novel? Does it interest you to develop that?

JAB: It does. However, I know that if I wrote another novel that I'd have to sit myself down and say, You need a plot, and a plot has not yet occurred to me. It didn't occur to me before either, and that's why I had such a hard time finishing *In Zanesville*.

SL: I found it so delightful.

JAB: Thank you. However, you've got to admit it didn't really have a plot. I'm not dissing it at all—I actually like that book, the relationship between those two girls meandering around their town.

SL: About a decade back, in *The New York Times*, Steve Almond wrote that his students were seeking ways to face the toughest truths within themselves so as to begin to make sense of them. How do you feel about the idea that writing memoir is therapeutic or can even lead to a catharsis?

JAB: I think the most therapeutic thing about writing is that it requires the writer to develop heightened skills at empathy, at projecting themselves into other people's lives, minds, and issues. That's actually the opposite of what we see a lot in memoir. In memoir writing, you have to seek to do something that's beyond self-discovery.

SL: Some have argued that there is too much confession in modern memoir.

JAB: I don't really care about confession. I don't even know quite what that word means in this context. What I think is that memoir is literature and literature is art and in art you must seek to illuminate something. Frequently, what I see as a teacher is untransformed suffering, where people just lay their sorrows and their anguish on the page. That might be therapeutic for them, but that's not art. If you're aiming toward art, you have to transform the suffering into something that makes it worthwhile for other people to read it.

SL: There's a notion that in confessional memoir, the pain feels raw and unprocessed, handing over that burden to the reader, who feels they have to somehow either console or accept it . . .

JAB: Right, you can't just put it out there in the world. You have to somehow transform it into art, and how do you transform anything into art? There are some things about the craft of writing that can get you there, but really it's magic. It's a kind of mystery that I don't even like to talk about where my own work is concerned, because I don't want to demystify it for myself.

SL: In her *The New York Times* review of *Festival Days*, Leah Hager Cohen wrote that because you wed intuition and observation, instead of calling you an essayist, we might call you a poet-naturalist. What do you think of this classification, and how would you prefer readers label the kind of writer you are?

JAB: I think that that [label] could be applied to Mary Oliver and Annie Dillard, so I would take it. Because I've taught [their work for] so long, I found it very touching to be even remotely linked. It made me love Leah.

SL: To be in such fine company.

JAB: Yeah, and for her to say something like that about my work. I spend forever laboring over sentences because I really care about words, phrases, sentences, paragraphs, sections, and whole essays. I craft those things to the point of no return, so to have somebody notice that really matters to me.

SL: What are your feelings about craft rules? What do you teach your students?

JAB: To break them whenever they can but also to be aware that they're breaking them. I try to teach them to challenge every sentence that they write. You have to think long and hard about what you're doing, and I'll tell you something about any essay that I've written: If you told me the first few words of any sentence in any essay, I could recite the rest of that sentence. I craft sentences as much as I write essays.

SL: Are you envious of prolific writers?

JAB: Yes!

SL: Do we hate them?

JAB: We hate them! They can go to a movie at night and have fun because

112 **BOOTH**

they did their work. Even when I've done my work, I have one sentence to show for it.

SL: It's an uneasy peace with your process?

JAB: Yes.

SL: One aspect of your writing that stands out is the attention to detail. How do you go about parsing this, either in your own writing or others' writing, to determine which details deepen a piece's overall meaning and which ones are extraneous?

JAB: Essays are small—if you want a detail, you have to make sure it has earned its place. You can't include everything, so if you're deciding to include something, it must work on several different levels at once. It needs to tell us about the story on the surface, and at the same time about the deeper story under the surface. And it should advance the story, too . . . that's three levels each sentence has to be doing for you. In an essay, you can't waste people's time.

SL: I love that you say that.

JAB: You can, a little bit, waste people's time with a novel, because people get in a novel and it feels roomy, and they just want to be there. So, you can linger here and there, and they'll have the patience to wait with you, to enjoy the milder scenery that goes by. In an essay or short story, however, you can't let them linger, it's all got to mean something.

SL: In an interview with Chelsea Hodson in *BOMB Magazine*, you spoke about reaching a certain age and "moving into the final phase," which makes me wonder about how this time of your life is for you, especially your relationship to ambition.

JAB: I used to be openly ambitious and forceful in terms of being my own best friend as a writer; I could put myself out there even when people were like, Sorry, we are not interested. Where that forcefulness comes from, I have no idea. I don't feel it in any other aspect of my life. Nowadays, literature and writing still matter to me more than anything else in the world; it's up there at the top. However, in terms of what I wanted to achieve, I've achieved it. I would love to immerse in a project again, but to tell you the truth, I spend a lot of my time teaching, and the older I get, the less energy I have for two full-time jobs.

SL: Is there a possibility that writing could become your full-time job instead?

JAB: Well, that will be wonderful someday. At some point it's about quality of life. I want part of my life to be about just being alive and thinking about what it means to be alive and be awake and aware. I would love to have that be half my life and the other half be writing.

SL: In an old interview with Stephanie Anderson for *Coastlines*, you stated that you valued your writing over your life. Can you explain what you meant by this, and do you still feel this way?

JAB: Yes, I still feel that way. Nothing in my life has ever mattered to me the way my writing has mattered to me, and I don't mean *my* writing, like this book or that book or this essay or that essay. I mean the endeavor of writing has meant more to me than anything else in my life.

SL: Is there such a thing for you as a guilty-pleasure read, something that's just fun but not nutritious or literary, whatever that means?

JAB: I just read a celebrity memoir. I'm reading *The Song of the Cell* by Siddhartha Mukherjee, David Quammen's *Breathless*, about Covid-19, and Matthew Perry's memoir, and all three were compelling to me. Two of them I barely understood, and with the Matthew Perry book, he couldn't stop telling us things that are either embarrassing, or that we already know. Like stop telling us how many millions of dollars you have—we already assume that about you. And apparently, you can't transform the suffering if you are a narcissist. I think I knew that already.

SL: Some people say that listening to audiobooks is cheating a little bit, that you lose something when you are not the one reading the words. What are your thoughts on this?

JAB: I listened to E. B. White read *Charlotte's Web*, and there's no better way to experience *Charlotte's Web* than through E. B. White's voice. I listened to *All Quiet on the Western Front* a decade ago. It's the best audiobook I have ever listened to. I think it's a separate

114 **BOOTH**

thing from reading a book on the page. I think you perceive it differently. Our attention spans are being formally and informally tinkered with all the time now, so reading a book on the page is very different. Multi-tasking just feels like tasking now.

SL: I loved your narration of *The Boys of My Youth*, and I'm curious why you didn't narrate *Festival Days*.

JAB: No, they're never going to let me do that again. Nobody liked it. You don't know what your voice sounds like, because you hear it from inside your head. My voice is sort of a soporific droning sound with very little inflection, which I knew, but I really fought [to do it].

SL: You wanted to?

JAB: I don't necessarily want someone's interpretation, even if it happens to sound better. But the publisher's concern, of course, is what works and what people want to buy.

SL: I have friends who don't want to listen to books that aren't narrated by the author.

JAB: I feel the same way. I have to listen to the sample to see if it's delivered in a way that allows me to feel like I'm reading. I don't like to hear it performed or interpreted.

SL: In a *CRAFT Literary* interview with Yvonne Conza, you wrote that you've learned from your students that it isn't the most gifted writer who succeeds. Can you tell me more about that?

JAB: It takes some kind of combination of having a gift and having certainty, which is part of ambition. You have to have energy, have to be able to accept rejection, which is an oxymoron, and have to be able to take from that rejection whatever you need to take from it. Sometimes, criticism is earned. Other times, you go, No, they're wrong. Both are helpful.

SL: Do your students ever bemoan the fact, especially for nonfiction writers, that in order to get a book deal, they've got to establish a platform, and a lot of the time that means they have to be active on social media?

JAB: I think that that is an excuse for people to be active on social media.

Beard   115

Nude

SAM FOUTS

—

fiction

WELL, IT WAS FRIDAY, AND ME, MIKE, KEI, ROSS, and Rod were going out to drink like we had been doing since undergrad. And 'cause Rod was getting evicted soon—said he couldn't pay rent being a street vendor anymore—he wanted to take us all to one of the cheaper places in his neighborhood, you know, before it wasn't his neighborhood anymore. And I guess we were all thinking, Why not, so we hopped on the train and met him across town over by the university.

Was a nice-looking area. That's what people typically said. I mean, the roads didn't have potholes and there were shops and old brick everywhere, students in nice clothes, but. It'd only been a few years since I'd graduated, and the place was so damn smooth now, sharp like they sanded it down with protractors—not a blade of grass splitting their sidewalks, and there were benches. Benches you couldn't sleep on and cops to make sure you didn't sleep under them, so I was thinking at the least it would be quiet around there, but hell. When we got there, the first thing we heard were sirens. And we saw them bouncing up and down the street by the campus, so we were thinking something crazy had to have happened, and we hurried over.

Well, we found Rod, found him watching some nude protestor getting arrested by like a dozen cops. She didn't have a sign—guess her body spoke for itself—and they were trying to get a towel over her, but she was fighting, and her legs were kicking and all dirty. It looked like she had run through some of the university's landscaping and uprooted a bunch of flowers. And Rod, his eyes were locked on her, and we were all thinking, Oh, man, he can't help himself, but when we went up to him to catch him red-handed, it's like there wasn't a drop of lust in this guy. I mean, he was smirking—like ear to ear—but he saw us and said nothing at first and just kept watching. Almost like he was impressed, 'cause then he started clapping, and it sure as hell wasn't for the cops, and even after they took that girl away, Rod still had that look. Like it was cut into him. And when everything was quiet again, he just turned to us and said there was a change of plans.

I mean, we were still drinking, only at a different venue. He'd said he had an idea, but it was bookstores and cafes all the way down, and hell, we were like drops on a canvas in that storefront glass, checking our balances and cards, just to be sure we could keep following. And Rod was telling us not to worry, but when we got there, you know, we were starting to worry 'cause the place's next to an old church that'd been made into a fancy-fucking-clothing place, and the bar itself was built into a vintage townhome.

Through the windows, I could see them putting dry ice in the drinks, lighting things on fire, getting all theatric even though that shit had like one shot in it. And for some reason, there was a bookshelf in the corner, and I was like, Are we even allowed in? But Rod, he stayed calm, said we were all good and ushered us forward, and the bouncer looked pissed at us, but hell. Let us in anyway and did it with a smile after Rod put twenty in his shirt pocket, but when we got inside, all their shit was also like twenty dollars—like motherfuckers had dresses on, button-up shirts, this wasn't a tavern or anything, so us in our hoodies and baggie jeans just decided to buy one drink each and take it slow, but Rod, he didn't buy shit. We were looking around, trying to figure out what his plan was, and then we saw him snatch a whole glass from a table, chug some, and then he came over and handed us the rest like he was Robin Hood or something. And he just looked at us and said,

Gentlemen.

And that was all. We were standing there for a few moments, kinda confused, so he went and stole another drink and did the same thing and yeah. After that, we got the idea, and it was going well, you know, like we were getting drunk, and everyone else was too drunk to notice what we were fucking doing, and we were making jokes and nobody was laughing, but we were having a good time anyway, and we were all getting bolder. Especially Rod. A few hours in, and he was acting like a show-off, taking a drink from one table, another from a different table, drinking them both while they spilled down his chin, then swapping them out for fresh ones, but oh, man: One of those times, he got real cocky, and this dude in like a white suit went to piss and had a whole drink just sitting there in front of the girl he was with. So, Rod went over and started chugging it, and the girl, she wasn't doing anything. She had a hand over her mouth, she was laughing, and we were, too, but, like, it was a big fucking drink, so before Rod could finish, the dude came back and saw Rod and went up and slapped him. But, Rod was so drunk, he just paused for a second then kept drinking, and the dude in the suit, he like stood back 'cause he didn't know what was happening, and Rod: He just looked at the guy and smirked. Then he took the rest of the drink and splashed it all over him, and this drink was red. Like *blood* red. And you could see it soaking right into the suit, so, yeah, the guy was pissed. He wasn't yelling or throwing a fit, but his mouth was clenched, and the drink was dripping off his face, which I thought was red *'cause* of the drink, but I realized the dude was embarrassed 'cause the girl he was with was laughing even harder now, like crying. And the guy, he looked like he wanted to say something, looked disgusted—at all of us—but he just walked away, grabbed the girl by the arm like she was a damn purse or something, and they got out of that place without a word. So, we just kept on drinking.

And eventually, closing time came around, and we were the only ones left, and the bartender was mopping, and there was basically just ice left in all of the cups, so we were getting ready to go. But, as we were leaving, the guy in the white suit was there. Right outside of the glass. And he was looking in. And he had a brand-new white suit on; no one could believe it. And he came through the door, real gentle. And his head was down like he didn't even wanna look at us, but *he* did—for a moment, he did—and he looked up and was ecstatic. Really grinning. And we were all frozen and nobody knew what do to, but he knew what to do, and he pulled out some fancy-looking pistol with an ivory handle and just shot Rod in the head.

And then he was off.

And we were just there.

Nobody was saying much. Nobody was saying *anything* at first, and the bartender, he was just mopping still, but you could tell he'd slowed down a bit. So then, we were all just looking at each other, and the bartender was looking at us every now and then, and his eyes were like *open* open, but his face was like a rock, lips straight. Expressionless—except those eyes, you know? 'Cause I don't think anyone there had ever seen that much blood before, and the only thing that got done, besides that mopping, was one of the guys throwing their hoodie over Rod's head, eyes closed the whole time like all the others. But not me.

Not me.

I saw it, I saw Rod's head, I saw the hole or whatever you wanna call it. And I didn't know if I should be grateful that his head wasn't blown off, because, hell, that may have been better, would've made it like a cartoon, and in a cartoon, his head would've just grown back from the stump of his neck, and we would've laughed about it. Instead, there was a crater. The shot didn't go out the other end, but it shattered the center of his forehead in an X, and from all the cracks, blood ran over his face in oily streams and chunks of flesh were bubbling to the surface, but you could still tell it was him, you know? Just changed. Broken. Not beyond recognition, but just above the threshold, and I felt like it was a mistake—a crime—like I shouldn't have seen it.

But, I did. And I wanted to see it again, and I don't know why, but I went on over and took the hoodie off, and all the other guys turned away, shouting for me to cover his head back up, but I wouldn't. I just kept looking at it, the wound, you know? And I'd never seen a brain before, but I was pretty sure I was looking at one then, and I kept looking, got closer and closer. And the others, they started asking the bartender what they should do, and he just looked at them and blinked, wrote his number on a receipt, and said the cops could reach him there if they needed him, and then he was out the door. So, everyone just took out their phones and started dialing 911, but I was still looking at Rod, and I saw then, saw it real clear all of a sudden that he was smirking under all that red. Ear to ear. And I just said, Stop. Like it was a sneeze, like vomit coming out of me.

And the others were all looking down at me—best they could—and they were looking at me like, What? But I was smiling then, and I looked at them and told them to put their phones down, and I said, We gotta do something, do something nice for Rod.

And Ross was like, Yeah, dude, a fucking funeral, and Mike and Kei started going on about how we'd pour beers on his grave—or if he was cremated, drink his ashes, like we talked about in high school—but I just shook my head.

I'm saying let's do something now.

And their eyes got really wide, and they were looking at me like, *Right now* right now? And I just kept smiling and went, What better time?

What better time?

* * *

Well, after that, I don't know. The guys stood there, thinking, and eventually, Kei came a little closer and started looking at Rod's head, too. His eyes widened, his breath got quick, but he stood there and couldn't stop looking, and he was shaking, but shit, he started smiling, too. And it looked like a nervous smile at first, but it just kept getting wider and wider, and then Ross and Mike joined, as well. They were covering their eyes, but you could tell they were peeking, 'cause all of a sudden, they bounced back, had to catch themselves. But, the longer they looked, the more fingers came down, and soon they were taking it all in, taking it in with me, and I think we all stood there over Rod's body for an hour, and nobody said anything. Was like we were all listening, you know?

To what, though? I couldn't tell you, but everyone was taking something in—like there was a voice coming from that wound—and after a while, I was thinking, Maybe we can call the cops now, maybe we've had our time, but I was looking at the other guys, and they were all nodding and looking at me, saying they wanted to do something now, too.

But, I didn't know what the fuck to do. And I didn't even know if being that close to a body was legal, but I was thinking for a good few minutes, thinking that we loved Rod, and we'd been to some funerals by then, funerals of real good friends, but I don't know. Even when the coffins were open, it never felt like you were saying goodbye. And I think the other guys were feeling it, too, 'cause next thing you know, we were wrapping Rod's head up with our hoodies and carrying him out the door, but I didn't have a plan or anything, so at first, we were just sneaking around with him on our shoulders, dodging cops down alleys on our way to the subway. But, then we crossed by the university again.

They hadn't cleaned up that protestor's mess, and the flowers were still scattered on the sidewalk, so I got everyone to put Rod on a bench, and I told them we needed decorations. So, we went over and started grabbing all the flowers, but we didn't stop with the ones that'd already been kicked up; we started snatching fistfuls of them right out of the mulch, and people were driving by, they were slowing and stopping and honking, calling us jackasses, but oh, man. We just kept grinning and picking the flowers, and eventually, we got like ten-bouquets worth all shoved into our pockets, pants, and hoods, then we made our escape down the street, and we were loud as dogs, so we had lights flickering on in all the lofts and curtains opening and silhouettes pointing, but nobody was sweating it, 'cause I think everyone was starting to feel something in those moments, something thawing. And maybe it was our pulses bubbling with adrenaline, but I'll tell you what: My heart had never felt that way before, 'cause really it wasn't a pulse; it was like nothing was beating at all, and hell, I think we forgot Rod was there, dead on our shoulders.

But oh, man, we sure remembered when we heard sirens dopplering our way, and we were off with Rod, running like nobody's ever run before, 'cause I don't know if any of us had really run—like *seriously* run—before that, but we were running then. And you should've seen our shadows playing in the sodium light all the way to the station. Down the stairs, over the platforms, without a spark in our heads, and it was like nobody thought we were holding a corpse, you know? 'Cause everyone was rolling their eyes when we ran by, steering clear, and they were probably thinking Rod was just drunk or this was a joke or something for TV, 'cause, like, who would do this? And I guess we were doing it, but shit, it doesn't mean it didn't feel real to us either, and in a flash, we were on the train without a problem. People all around us, people sitting feet from Rod, but they didn't see his blood, didn't see his head, and we were quiet then. So, they were, too.

Since I lived closest to the stop, we carried Rod's body up to my apartment, and I let everyone in, went straight to the bathroom, and started running some water. Next thing you know, we got Rod in the tub. Naked. And I don't think I'd seen him like that since our mommas used to bathe us together, but it felt right. Felt natural. And nobody was wincing anymore when we washed the blood off his face—all of us just in there, running our hands over his skin, soap on his chest and thighs and all over until we'd groomed every last part of him.

Then, I went out into the kitchen and grabbed a bottle of that cheap wine he loved and had everyone take a swig, and when it'd gone around, I gave the rest to Rod and poured it all over his face before we took him out of the bath and set him on my bed. And blood was getting all over my pillows and blankets, but I could just buy more, I could just buy more, and we tucked the covers around him and wrapped some flowers in his palms, scattered the rest over the sheets and carpet, and when we finished, we walked out of the room, and I shut the door behind me, but before I did, before I did, I swear I saw the petals glowing in his hands, sprouting from their wilted shapes, singing through their lethargy. Even for just a little longer. Then, the door closed quietly, and after that, I only remember waking up the next morning. Sober.

The wine bottle was still on the table, so we all knew it wasn't a dream. And one by one, we started clustering around my bedroom, looking at the door, not really knowing what to do even when everyone was there. I got sweat all over my hands, Mike and Ross were on their knees and praying, and I remember Kei was just standing there. His head on his feet. And he said nothing, and I said nothing, and for an hour, we just idled and bounced between the narrow hall, until eventually, I went up and opened the door. Eyes closed. And I walked in and counted to three and opened my eyes, and there was Rod. His skin was all pale, mouth was hanging open just a crack, but his eyes were closed, and he looked nice. Looked comfortable. And Mike and Ross were praying again, and me and Kei were on our knees, too, and we were crawling all over, climbing up the sheets, and looking over the body, looking for an answer, looking into the hole in his head, looking for light in his eyes, looking, looking for something, for color, for anything.

But, Rod was silent, and I said that maybe he was just sleeping this one off, and we all started howling, we started rolling on the ground and pounding the carpet with our fists, and we were coughing, trying to catch our breaths, and tears were streaming down our faces, and for the first time, I was wondering if you could die from laughing so hard.

But you know what? When the chuckles faded out, and we could only hear the cars outside, all of us started crying. Started sobbing. And nobody cared about the snot in their noses or how they sounded, and we touched Rod's hair and touched his skin and talked with him for hours, talked and talked and talked and told stories and didn't stop even when we got thirsty, even when we had to piss, even when the cops came in and put us in cuffs, 'cause it felt good.

It felt damn good.

Afternoon at the Wig Shop

CLAIRE STANFORD

—

fiction

ONE AFTERNOON AT THE WIG SHOP, A BIRD-LIKE woman enters, a gauzy lavender scarf wrapped around her bald head, the cloth flecked with silver. She is pale and thin, the chemotherapy making her wilt. Her clothes hang loosely from her body.

The wig-shop owner, a stout woman with a formidable chest, speaks to the bird-like woman in a gentle voice, pointing to a curly blond wig and then a wavy black one and then a straight red bob she says would go nicely with the bird-like woman's hazel eyes. The woman nods even though she is not a redhead.

Yes, that one, she says. Let's try that one. Only . . . The woman looks around. No one is in the shop but her and the owner and the mannequins. The walls are lined with mirrored glass, the mannequins' heads reflecting back at her from all angles. She studies them for a moment, their staring faces. At the front of the shop are two large windows that face onto the sidewalk, allowing anyone to look in. Do you have somewhere more private?

Of course, honey, the owner says. She takes the woman to the back room, which is cluttered with cardboard boxes and broken display tables. There's one mirror, leaning against some half-filled shelves, in a large gilded frame.

The owner lingers, as if she is reluctant to leave the bird-like woman alone, but the woman says, Thank you, her voice firm. Her voice is still firm, even if her body is frail. She waits until the owner has closed the door, and then she steps in front of the mirror and takes a long look.

When she is feeling more upbeat, she tries to make a joke of her appearance, telling her husband that she looks like a baby dinosaur, freshly hatched. He tells her of course she doesn't, that she looks beautiful, but she prefers the baby dinosaur to beautiful. Beautiful is what you tell a person who has no hair, who has only scars where her breasts used to be.

Something in the mirror catches her eye. The corners are streaked with grime and dust, but behind the smudges she thinks she sees a face. She feels her heart speed up as she turns, but it is just another mannequin head sitting on the shelf. The nose has broken off. It has no wig.

You and me, she says to the head.

She looks back to the mirror and begins the slow process of unwinding her scarf, wrapping the folds of fabric around her hand as she goes, revealing her bare skull inch by inch. She places the scarf on one of the few empty surfaces and picks up the red wig. She is lifting it to her head when she hears a voice behind her.

No, don't.

Her heart speeds up again, and she turns to the door, but it is still closed. She looks around the room, but everything is as it was: the haphazard stacks of boxes, the dusty beam of sunlight, the stray mannequin head, tilted slightly askew. She turns back to the mirror, her fingers looping through the smooth netting on the underside of the wig as she again raises it to her scalp.

Please, the voice says, leave it off.

This time, the woman whirls around too fast, the dim room swirling for a moment before it steadies. Still, there is no body, no movement.

The woman scans the room again, more slowly now. The plastic head sits on the same place on the shelf, but its eyes seem to have shifted slightly. She turns back to the mirror.

Please, she hears the voice again, I've never seen anyone who looked like me before.

Let me see your body, it says.

The woman hesitates, looking away from the face.

Show me what you look like, the mannequin says, insistent. I want to see.

The woman pauses for a long moment. Over the past several months, so many people have seen her naked body—the doctors, the nurses, the lab techs—but to them, it is only one misbehaving body out of many misbehaving bodies, the casing for a problem to be solved. They treat her as if she is an anatomical model, one of their classroom dummies. They mark up her flesh with dotted lines: cut here.

Her husband sees her body, too, of course: when she is changing, the few times they've been able to make love. When her shoulder hurts, he helps her in the bath, but he looks away when it is time to soap her chest. He acts like he is not looking away, but she can tell that he is, can feel him flinch as the sponge meets her sternum.

She wishes her husband would talk to her like this voice, this voice that wants so badly to see her naked form. She wishes her husband would grab her, like he did in the old days and kiss her all over, his lips on her flesh, on places that no other lips had ever touched: her hip, her butt cheek, behind her knee.

Now, he is afraid that if he kisses those places, he will break them, that if he touches her, she will shatter.

She looks again at the mannequin's face in the mirror then nods and puts down the wig. She unbuttons her shirt, sloughing it off her bony shoulders and letting it drop to the ground. Her chest is covered by a cream cotton bra, no wires, the kind she remembers begging her mother to buy her when she was eleven and her breasts were only starting to come in.

Keep going, the voice says. Please.

She reaches around her back and unclips the clasp. She closes her eyes and lets the bra too fall to the floor. She cannot look at what her chest has become, at the X'd-out scars across what used to be her nipples, the concavity of her solar plexus, the neat stacking of her protruding ribs. She feels a phantom pain in her breasts, the breasts that no longer exist, and she wonders if the mannequin feels this same pain in the body it has never had.

When she finally opens her eyes, she does not look at her body, at the reflection of the body that is her body but is not her body, but instead at the face in the mirror. It is watching her intently, its eyes wide.

I wish I could know what it is to have a body, says the voice.

The woman hesitates. She turns. She walks to the shelf where the mannequin's head sits immobile.

Go ahead, it says.

The woman picks up the mannequin's head, the plastic smooth and cool on her palm. She is careful not to touch the mannequin's face—not to stick a finger in its nose or eye. She holds it gently by the base of its neck, where the plastic flattens out, waiting for a body to support it.

She walks back to the mirror. She faces the glass and lifts the mannequin's head in front of her own. The woman cannot see the image in the mirror; the mannequin's head blocks her view.

Describe it to me, the woman says. Tell me what you see.

It's what I've always wanted, says the voice. A body of my own.

There is a noise out in the hallway, a clattering of objects. The woman freezes. But the noise subsides.

All right, the woman says. Time to put you back.

But, when she tries to lower the head, her hands feel only her own cheeks, her own chin. She tugs harder, but still the mannequin's head will not budge. She twists her torso to look at the mirror from a different angle, but still she cannot see her face. She sees only the face of the mannequin, its broken nose, looking strangely at home on her body. Is the mannequin's face now her face? Somehow, this thought doesn't induce any panic, only a strange wave of relief.

Isn't this what you want? the mannequin says. If you give me your body, you will always be safe.

The woman thinks about the look on her husband's face when he accidentally catches sight of her scars.

It won't hurt, the mannequin says. Not at all. You've been through so much pain, I know. This will not be anything like that.

She feels her body beginning to stiffen. She can no longer move her arms, no longer move her feet. The voice speaks soothingly to her, and she does not feel scared. She feels the same way she felt in the seconds after the anesthesia entered her veins, before everything became black.

She could stay here forever. No more pills, no more tubes. A body, permanent, unchanging.

The woman hears a knock on the door. She feels a sudden pain at her neck, like the pins and needles when your foot falls asleep but amplified by a thousand. The pain sears through her, soaring through her fragile body. She has grown so accustomed to pain. It does not shock her; it only wakes her. Wakes her to this body that is still her body, this body that she is not ready to give up on, not yet.

With one great tug, the woman pulls the mannequin's head away. The voice is quiet as she puts the head back on the shelf, its eyes unblinking.

One second! she calls, slipping her shirt back over her head, smoothing it across her breastbone.

She hurries past the wig-shop owner, thanking her for her time, no wig today.

Tonight, she will pour an entire bottle of bubble bath into the tub.

She will lower her body into the eucalyptus heat.

And when her husband tries to look away, she will hold his face, gently, by the chin.

She will take his hand and press it to her chest.

Eumorpha Achemon; My Exoskeletal Self-Defense
Willow James Claire

testosterone thick & viscous floods my mouth
most days my wrists are sphinx-moths pink
hindwings glimmering between daytime moon & a feeling
my throat bubbles apples plump & sweet
unchrysalis, am I animal or tool
I spend most days picking backfeathers like pimples
the whetstone & the blade   predator & the prey
even blood looks ugly when wet on an efficient spade
no plastic nails despite my plastic human wishes
instead, thick skin through thick sharp skin
little viscera of me scattered around footsteps & lye
a flit of wing or slit of silken thread down the leg
of a black dress   but cut implies blood   but blood implies
a lineage   the fittest wear their hiding well   that thin survival
shadowed in softgreys that fur the body as part of the night
for a handsome thing I know so little what I am
a lifespan   a beastworm edging inches toward a meal
my mouth never stops moving for fear of what hunger can hide
a man leers with net intention   I pink my abdomen
for a monstrous thing I feel so much pain
while offense makes each meal & daynight cycle a kind
of waiting   what have I to lose except a life   a safety
my mother has never killed in my name   what violent shame
my father would never kill in my name   what violent shame
most days my bodies sleep between dying reborn leaves
I barely wanted   where have I to fly
except my loom   a mirror
of skin stitched screamingly in the quiet dark   & when I wake
I'll have changed   no   I'll remain the same   a trembling prey

(Heavy Metal) Boots
Naomi Leimsider

How the heft of the heels, the hook and eyes, the being all zipped in pebbled, pitted animal skin reduced my once functioning whole to disfigured parts. How my high arches—those delicate hills under pretty little feet—collapsed flat, timeworn, stressed out from the strain of raised veins and mangled muscles. How hammered toes, hairline broken tiny bones, and long ago stunted growth plates in uncreased tanned hide waiting for the wrinkles of wear, of time, to wriggle in. How I pulled the laces tight, so tight, those stripped frayed strings, so thick black sock blood stuck to flayed heels and bubble blisters leaking liquid—such sweet white sap of friction—smelled good, so good, like musty insides, like organic rot. The persistent agony of wanting to put them on again. Bouts of deep need. To pull them. Slow and tight. So tight. Around now scarred ankles; up, up fat varicose legs; over the border of shredded knees; and remember how they edged—teased—the bottom of my black spandex skirt. How I want them still. How easy it was to break this body. How now I know. How I loved—love—the way they hurt.

Mimaw Burning Sage
Erin Pinkham

Burying pancakes in whipped cream, Mimaw told me of the ways to rid a ghost, cause my *Pop-Pop was the meanest fucking one* she had ever dealt with. It had been nine months since they moved into this house after the state built a six-lane highway through their old living room. It had been eight months since he died on the kitchen floor, rolling on his back like a June bug, mouth foaming. She told me to search, under couch cushions, in Pop-Pop's jars of coins, her purse, my purse, to find all the pennies we could. We bought sixty cans of salt at the Mad Butcher and started with them. Spilling their contents in her yard, over daylilies, under the chain fence, past dead birds the dog collects, then inside over windowsills and thresholds. All the while, she placed a penny in every corner of the house: the laundry room, the kitchen, the living room, the bathroom, the guest bedroom, her room, her bedroom, and even in the backs of closets. She bundled sage in her shaky hands, as small and wrinkled as a coin purse. She lit the perennial plants and chanted. This is my house. You are not welcome. *This is my house now, you are not welcome, Gordon. This is my house, damn it, you are not fucking welcome.* This was not the first time I watched her rid his ghost. She had scrubbed the floors, sold his truck, his boots, and books. She had drowned in the bottles of Wild Turkey that he used to hide at the bottom of the kitchen pantry. She took down the wedding photo—veil sticking out of her beehive, gappy tooth grin, his hand gripping the back of her neck. But, still, a year later, in her backyard, Mimaw will stir the fire until

she buries embers
of damp leaves and hollow sheets,
below the blue ash.

epigenetics or: hope for easeful adaption

nicole v basta

a sparrow lands on the barbed wire
and drops like a stone
how many generations until
we learn to pick the post instead

i go on living like what else is there
but time to count, ease to hope for

it's a friday night, apocalypse outside
and the silty river in me rushes
with melted snow—ancestors
kneel, huddle, wring the clothes

past the fence and a few beats
above silence is the sound
of what we call witness

out here, it is nothing
to glimpse loopholes
in time's passing

two women take all fours
in a field, match the crowns
of their heads

like the slow pose of eden
this kneeling collapses
both yesterday and centuries
after our children are dead

a version of this myth
puts birds on their backs
in another, a mirror is painted black

in yet another, a handless woman
balances a pear on her lips
did you turn to her
or was it a trick?

the husk of illusion
about *passing on* sings along

what crouches in our bones
we will never truly know

like the sparrow, i am learning
to land on the post

like the post, every year, i look
a little more like the earth

The Rage Room

MIALISE CARNEY

—

fiction

MY DAUGHTER OXANA WILL NOT STOP CALLING ME at work. From anywhere inside the rage room, I anticipate the ring, the tiny hairs on my forearms standing up while I'm sorting intake, when I'm scrubbing the floors, in the moment before I exit through the back door toward the dumpster to throw away battered planks and cushions. Since I left my husband almost a year ago, she has turned greedy, needing too much attention and comfort for a girl of fourteen. I feel it in my stomach, the wet-oatmeal weight of Oxana's nervousness and my want to detach myself from her, in the lull of cleaning. Every day, inside the cavern of my chest, a rubber band pulls tighter, waiting for the giddy-electric right moment to let go.

Behind the heavy metallic door, a man's dull scream escapes, accompanied by the faint sound of shattering, crystal skittering across the floor. I stand by with my cart, worry the chemical-dry skin around my nails, wait for the foghorn that announces when his time is up and when I can go inside and begin cleaning up the mess. I love the rage room, the gulf between the mess they make and the fixing I do, how the smashing bridges our separate lives together like thread. Company policy says that women aren't allowed to rage inside the rage room, but we're allowed to clean it, so of course I have settled with that.

The lobby telephone startles me with the same indulgence of my morning alarm, and I listen to Nika's soft murmuring to see if it's Oxana or a client checking up on their appointment. I have told my daughter a hundred times, Do not call me at work unless you want to go hungry, Do not call me at work if you love me, but she doesn't listen, she rings any time she likes.

I look at the clock above the door, blinking down the seconds until the end of this man's session. Down the hall, Nika calls to me, "Maggie, it's for you."

Our secretary, Nika, is a daft little thing, all elbows and skirts and *how can I help you* and watery-eyed smiles. During the day, I avoid her, but she catches me between my work to ask me, to beg that I let her see inside. The rage room only attracts a particular type of woman, a woman who yearns for more space than she's allowed. It's not nice of me, but I don't tell her. I seal my lips up tight, I pretend I could never sneak her in, I could never tell her the secrets. I like how she quivers with want, how I have the power to decide how long it eats her up.

I leave my cleaning cart by the door where I'm folding rags still warm from the dryer into neat, little squares. I lean against the side of the desk, press the receiver to my ear—it smells a little like disinfectant. "What?" I say, firm but quiet because I know Nika is listening even though she bends her neck and scrolls up and down on the same too-bright page of her computer screen out of respect for my privacy. Sometimes, I think she's embarrassed by my inability to control my daughter, the only thing in the world I should be able to control.

"Mama," Oxana's voice crinkles through the phone. She is in that awful place I remember, the chasm between child and adult and how awful it is to cross it with no safety nets underneath. "My stomach hurts."

I shift on my warm ankles as Oxana relents the trials of her morning. I tell her not to call me at work, that I could lose my job, but I can't help but feel a thin relief settle on my shoulders when I hear her gravelly voice, that she is alive, unhurt, and needy, that she calls me and not my ex-husband. Her call is long and winding, beginning with her stomach and concluding with some vague mentions of girls and their meanness, the sharpness of their tongues and their eyes. I twist the sticky cord on the phone until her voice grows distant and crackly, until I'm alone with Nika's nervous breathing and the sound of the man smashing his way through the room.

When I let go, her voice bounces back sharp like the mewl of a kitten. "Oxana, you act like a child. I will be home in the evening. You must manage until then," I say. Before I disconnect, I instruct her again on how long to boil water for her favorite rhubarb tea.

Nika takes the phone from me and places it too gently behind the desk. I thank her just as the foghorn sounds, and she nods and looks towards the door. In the quiet, I know what she wants but is too meek to say: I must get back to work.

The man lets out one final wail, a siren on the shore mourning the thing she loved and then drowned. I walk quickly back to my closet, ready my cart, wait for the final click, the sound of the door releasing before I can enter the rage room and begin cleaning up the mess.

The door clicks. I pull on my gloves. I open the door and roll my cart inside.

I breathe in the faint twirling of dust, glass shards, and spittle, the sweet earthy smell of sweat lingering in the air. I feel the heat, the coiling, ever-amounting disgust for my daughter, leave my body green in slivers alongside the particles, the asbestos-and-woodchip release of the last client's pain.

I let the heavy metal door close behind me with a satisfying clip. I step over thin shards of glass that tinkle like snow beneath my shoes. I pick up my broom and sweep. I lose time in the cleaning, pick up shards of vases, planks of splintered wood, green and red cracked ceramic plates. I stuff broken canvas paintings and shreds of paper into a large stretchy trash bag. I admire the tender teeth marks in plastic fruit, heavy with the memory of a muffled scream. I spot-clean the floors, the walls, the blinking green digital clock that counts down the minutes before each forty-five minute session is up. It's the only thing behind bulletproof glass—it had been shattered too many times. Inside the rage room, behind the thick steel door, I can't hear the ring of the phone. I am utterly alive and alone.

I set up the new items, the rows of vases, ceramics, and wooden planks, stacks of papers, cushions, and fresh pencils to snap. I prop up the dummy woman—I named her Sylvie—and brush her sickly yellow hair behind her flat plastic ears. I pity the fleshy realness of her arms. How cold they are, but how alike Oxana's. Her arms are still girlish and easy to pinch with my fingers when she is naughty, despite how fast she wiggles from my reach.

With twenty seconds to spare, I roll my cart out the door and back into my closet. I catch only a glimpse of the next man checking in at the counter, jitteriness in his shoulders shaking his carefully gelled hair. In his nervousness, he reminds me a little of my husband, my ex-husband, I suppose I should say. It has been nearly eleven months since I left him, but sometimes I still slip into old habits. Sometimes, when I wake up in the middle of the night, I can feel the weight of his hand on my thigh, his snoring just above my right ear.

I scratch the skin dry on my arms. The faint buzzer sounds, locking the man into the room. Before him, so much opportunity: what to

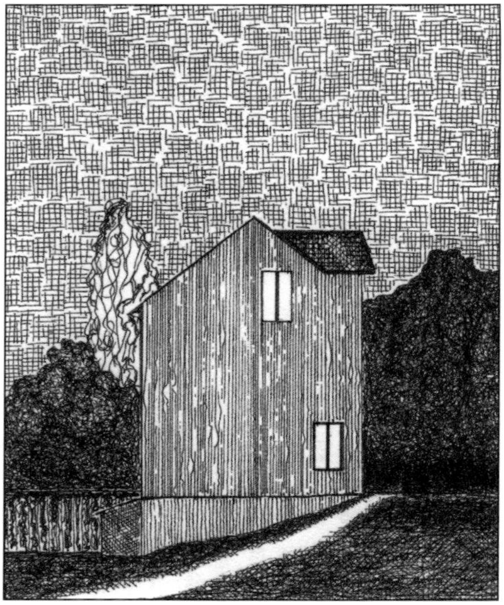

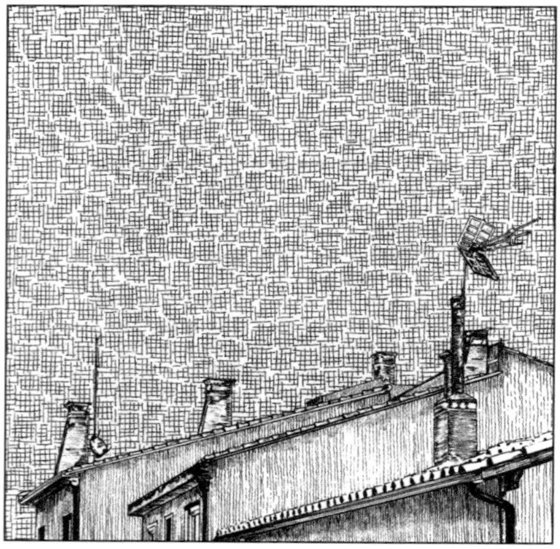

choose first, holding them, testing the weight of an object and what it will sound like, what it will feel like to start and how much it will hurt to stop. Inside the supply closet, I snap on the light and get to work resetting my cart for the next cleaning. I have forty-five minutes to prepare.

Oxana has not forgiven me for leaving her father, though I tell her it was for the good of us both, our need for quiet and less violence, less drunken nights and strange women hiding underneath my bed. In his absence, her memory of him grows fonder, softer, the dry sting of scoldings replaced by warm afternoons eating sandwiches by the pond, the soft-lavender sweetness of flowers after a recital, dancing around the kitchen to music scratching through the radio. In his place, I grow monstrous, controlling, and ever-tired—I am the woman she will resist and become anyway.

She thinks I do not know what it is like to be a girl, the unfairness of the body and the need to curl up the little animal of yourself into a dark mossy ball, push it into the depths of your stomach. I remember fourteen easily, the frustration of watching the other girls lengthen into tall willowy bodies and perfect icicle wrists, how good they were at shifting into women, how eagerly they attracted the boys, while I felt uncomfortable in my misshapenness, too small and hungry for my own good.

I was embarrassed of my own mother and her weakness, the kitchen grease spotted across her skin and how she tended endlessly to my brothers with more care than she provided me. I stayed out later, in the woods, in my friends' gardens, after school to avoid her like a mirror, the way she began to grow redder and more bent with work. My father, in contrast, was stoic; he never raised his voice at me or told me I was brutish and unremarkable. I watched as my brothers grew bigger and he guided them to the rage room to teach them all the ways to expel the unruliness of their bodies, while my mother slapped my hands for fidgeting, for uncrossing my legs.

Once I had Oxana, I thought often about how little I missed my mother. The only thing I could picture were her hands.

Oxana is so much like me. I think that is why we fight. In our apartment, I watch her play woman, roll the waistband of her skirt over to shorten it, cross her legs at the ankle, call me *Mother* instead of *Mama*, roll her eyes when she thinks I cannot see her in the reflection of the window above the sink. I love her the most in these moments where she falls short, where she slurps when she drinks a glass of juice and forgets not to cross her fingers when she says "I love you" at night. I want to keep her small and animal; I don't want her to yet learn how to pretend to be something else for the rest of her life.

Around mid-afternoon, I am slow cleaning the room—unacceptable to cut into some man's time, but it is not always so easy. The man before made an awful mess, smashed everything into a fine, sparkling dust that coated furniture and the floor, so I had to take everything out and start again. He had jammed nails into poor Sylvie's eyes and bit a whole chunk from her squidgy plastic arm that he must have swallowed, because I couldn't find the other piece.

I exit a few minutes late. A man stands by the door, his thin body shifting in a too-large gray suit. He is short with his arms wide out holding the frame, trying to look commanding. I find his boyishness almost endearing.

"Take your time, sweetheart," he says.

I look down at his dull shoes, hold my cart still and wait for him to move. I don't speak with the clients unless necessary. I am not paid to grovel like Nika.

He makes a dry noise in his throat. "Better be good as new, then, or I'll have a talk with your boss. I think you could use a good talking to."

My organs itch, and I feel a prickling in my muscles. I push my cart closer, imagine shoving him, his tiny boy-body folding in the middle, dropping to the floor like a wet sack of laundry. Unconscious, blood tricking out the side of his thin, weepy lips.

He finally slides out of the way enough for me to push by. "Smile, it can't be so bad," he says, his hand moving along the sweaty small of my back, pinching the fleshy part of my hip.

Outside, I stand in the cold. I breathe heavily, so I start to feel light-headed. I swim through my rage. I throw everything, one by one, over my head and into the dumpster, the loud thumps of items slamming against the rusty metal sides, clinking beautifully against other broken things. The sounds please me, tickle sweet my eardrums like a cotton bud scratching the unreachable cavern of my skull, relief dancing down the length of my spine. I throw until my arms ache, until I feel quite like Sylvie, beat and battered, on my way out.

I toss eyeless Sylvie over last. I brush back her hair one final time, the yellow strands itchy and dry on my skin. I have often thought of Sylvie as a daughter, and I feel lucky that she can't tell me how much it hurts.

I plant a tiny kiss on Sylvie's forehead, and then I heave her over my head into the dumpster. She arcs beautifully, dives in like a swimmer to her unforgiving end. I will see her again in another form, fresh from the packaging. I am happy that for her I can start again, I can hold her clean and unknowing.

I retrieve a new Sylvie from the supply closet and carry her into the rage room. The door clicks; it's my time to clean the awful man's mess, and I find he left me a tiny heart, made of red ceramic plate shards, on the floor. Something dark squeezes my stomach like a fist, and I crunch the heart under my heel until it is dust.

***

The closet door opens a crack, and Nika's face sticks through. "Oh, sorry, Maggie," she says. Her eyes dart like jumping beans, like any part of my body is too awful to settle upon for more than a moment. At first, I fear she is going to say I have a phone call, and a little electric jolt of shame zips through my organs from my spine to my naval.

"I just had a question. Can I ask you a question?" she says. She slimes into the closet before I say yes, the door coming to rest on the precipice of her hip. I feel her breath, strawberry sweet, tickle the fuzz across my upper lip.

"What is it?" I ask, backing up a step. The edge of the wooden shelf presses sharply against my back, and I feel the sharp bite of a splinter wiggling its way in.

"Maggie, you know how important it is for me to be available for our clients during working hours," she says. I watch a loose eyelash hang from the lid, cutting through the center of her pupil. "It's not easy to be productive with so many distractions," she says.

Nika holds her hands below her chest and twirls her fingers at the joints so methodically I wonder if she hopes they will pop clean off. When I think of Oxana as a woman, I hope that she is nothing like Nika. I would like Oxana to be like Sylvie, to be stoic and large, unyielding. I want her to be able to sit through everything that comes at her without flinching, without bending like a tree towards the ground.

Nika continues, "It can be very good to focus on work and leave everything else at the door." She smiles wide, her little jagged teeth white and shining with the glow of the single bulb.

Leave everything at the door. How wonderful, how easy that all would be, to reach my hands down deep into my lungs, my stomach, the depths of my pelvis, the aching parts around my toes, and pull out my burdens, leave them in a bloody heap by the door to be retrieved warm and buzzing after hours in the sun. How I wish my burdens hadn't burrowed, like parasites or tumors braided into the fiber of my muscles.

"I'm not sure what you mean," I say. I press the plastic edge of the broom into my palm, feel the dull electric resistance of my nerves.

Nika resettles her shoulders, her eyes flicking back underneath her fringe, searching her eye sockets for the right way to tell me I am bothering her, I am not doing my work. This is not the first time Nika and I have had this talk—though she has only gotten more confident, before, she nearly cried when she asked me to stop letting my daughter call me at work. I can't tell her I have little control over my daughter or maybe that I like to hear her voice.

"I spoke with Boss the other day about our jobs and how important they are. He agreed we shouldn't be distracted."

I feel a hot stone in my stomach, sending warm vibrations through my body, across the expanse of my back. I can feel it too, my hands clenching into aching fists by my sides and across my dim field of vision, flashes of another future where I can't stuff it, I can't swallow my pride. It's fast, the feeling of violence in my throat and my hands and how easily they could collide with her warm rounded cheeks, how they'd redden with the sting of my palms.

I flatten my sticky hands against the front of my pale smock. I smile and thank her in a clear voice for reminding me of my place and what I'm good for and what I'm not.

"Oh, I'm so glad you understand," she says, and she hugs me tightly over the shoulders. The foghorn sounds outside, releasing me from her grasp as she totters out to the lobby, pulling down the hem of her too-tight skirt.

I roll my cart out of the closet. I wait by the door until I hear the click, until I can go inside and begin cleaning up the mess. I imagine Oxana, her needs and how I cannot control her, how most days I don't want to stop her from calling, from trying to tell me all that is crawling around inside her. She will understand one day, I know. I only wish it would all come sooner.

The door clicks. I roll my cart inside and close the door. The destruction unfurls before me. I bite into the squishy part of my hand to keep from kneeling down before it like an altar, to keep from crushing it into a fine powder with my palms.

I can't be slow again. I pull out my dustpan and begin cleaning. Without the rage room, without this rage, Oxana and I would have nowhere to go.

With three seconds to spare, I roll the cart out. Before I have even cleared the doorway, Nika's bob swings in my direction. "Maggie," she says, "The phone." I can feel it in my joints, an awful squeaking quelch, like I am turning to soup where I stand. I take the receiver and press it to my ear.

"Oxana, you must stop calling me at work," I say.

"Maggie, it's me." My husband's voice simmers through the line; so unlike Oxana's gravelly voice, it's warm, it's wet, and I can feel it wrapped around my biceps, my throat.

"You must do something about Oxana," he says, and I can imagine him, his curls and the way he twirls his tie around his finger, pulling tight, the blood pooling thick and brown in the pad of his thumb. "She cannot keep calling me at work."

He continues, but I'm not listening. I can feel it, the energy, the little rubber band in my chest, pulling tight, fraying. I can't stand it, Oxana and her neediness, him calling me after all this time, at work, digging his jagged nails into my skin. Why is it always my job to be the one in control, while he can follow the whims of his heart and his fists, and I need to keep Oxana and myself from stretching beyond the containers of our bodies, from snapping out of place. And all I want is the silence, the electric, stoic monotony of the rage room. I don't want to clean up any other kind of mess.

Husband's voice crinkles, "Oxana has asked to live with me. Is that what I must do?"

It happens before I'm ready, the spilling over. It starts somewhere fast and hot in my chest, right beneath the bones of my ribcage, then it comes down my arms, shoots through my legs, and then I'm grabbing the pamphlets on Nika's desk, tearing, ripping through the thick stacks with my teeth. It tastes so good, the ripping, flakes of paper stick to my tongue, so I spit, I cough. Something deep and awful inside me tears out, a guttural howl, animal, I think, beast. I clear the desk with my arms, revel in the stinging pain in my elbows, the slaps of my hands as colored pens and perfect stacks of sticky notes stutter, tumble to the floor. I grab the cool lamp, smash it, and the glass bulb disintegrates in sparks of mercury over the tile—I breathe them in gladly like little stars.

I hear faint whimpering, Nika cowering by the door, and I don't care. I kick the desk again and again, shocks of pain numbing my toes. Oh, that release of my body from myself: I float from the floor, I ring myself out like the kitchen sponge. I am unstoppable, I am strong. I stretch my fingers until the dry palms of my hands ache; I tear through fabric, smash through glass paintings on the wall. Shards stick in my knuckles; I push them in deeper, become one with the outside, bone-andbloodandearth mixing. Primordial soup. I am running through the woods; I am howling and wild and endless and so so angry. Everything comes up and out like vomit, hot and painful, breathless but necessary. Husbandoxanamamagirlsgirlsgirls, all of it in my screaming, my tearing through the room. And I am running, I am completely, endlessly free.

***

Oxana sits across from me on visiting days in the hospital. She plays with her fingers, and I stare at her knees, too pale and dry. I ask her if she's eating enough. She shrugs and pulls at the pleats in her skirt. They won't lie flat, and I can tell her Papa's new wife is not very skilled at ironing.

I have felt very dumb since I've been here, dull and embarrassed and ashamed, though that's not enough to prove to the doctors I am capable of change, that I will be better. I've told them in our weekly sessions, between all the staring out the barred windows and doing impossible puzzles, that it was a mistake, that I snapped, but they frown and say that's exactly what they're concerned about. A bout of hysteria, they've decided, but they haven't told me what I need to do to prove that I will keep it all tucked up inside this time. So, I stay quiet, I cross my ankles when I sit, and I smile all the time and bat my eyelids. I'm not sure how much longer I will last, tittering and apologizing, playing Nika twelve hours a day.

I do feel sorry for Nika. She is such a nervous girl, trying so hard to be exactly what everyone wants and expects but never getting it quite right. I wonder if she still works at the rage room or what new Maggie has rolled into my place, if she's any good at sweeping and cleaning and if Nika likes her better, if she fits nicely into all of my spaces. I imagine that she looks just like me, this woman who slipped into my uniform and who sweeps and scrubs and cleans the glorious mess, tucks it into a tight little trash bag, throws it away without a thought. They should make a monument, I think. A piece of modern art. The Man Unrestrained. Unraveled.

Oxana shifts uncomfortably across from me. I am not allowed to touch her, which I don't think is right. It's difficult to watch her collar, how it crinkles up on one side. "Are you happier now with your Papa?" I ask. "You always said all the things he would get for you."

She shifts in her seat, nearly puts a finger in her mouth but reconsiders, tucks her palm under her thigh. "Yes," she says. "I get all that I like."

I know she is lying by the warm flush of her cheeks, the bugginess of her eyes that wander along the dirty grout of the floor. She is shifting from girl into woman more starkly each week—she has begun to think more deeply about others than herself.

I want to go home to my daughter. I want to fix it, mold the dirt with my fingers. But the doctors worry in whispers to my ex-husband when he comes to retrieve Oxana from the visits. *We do not think she fully understands the gravity of her behaviors. She may never be the good wife and mother you once had.*

I watch Oxana shift beside him, how she picks at a scab on her arm and sucks on her hair, the way his limp arm wraps around her shoulders, how he kisses her head and I'm not allowed to touch her, how I may never be her mother again.

My ex-husband is eager for me to be released so I can retrieve Oxana, so he can pay attention to his new, pregnant wife.

The problem is she is simply too fragile, the doctors say. But the problem is I'm enormous, I'm strong, I'm kinetic. I could tear more than rooms; I could tear whole worlds apart with my teeth.

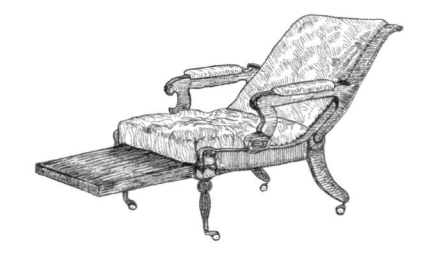

Girlhood Pentaptych

K.S. DYAL

nonfiction

I. FOREST LAWN

I don't know why we hung out in the cemetery, tank tops dusting mausoleum walls in the sleepy heat, except that maybe while eating Twizzlers and discussing our code-name system for boys—from attractive (Swans) to not attractive (Crumpets) and various in between (e.g., Monets: only attractive from afar)—we thought angels would come for us, stepping quiet-footed through the grass to sweep us up to a heaven without mirrors. Years later, I'd find photos from one of those afternoons, and our faces would be sunlit smirks. Scrawny bodies slouched, a headstone behind each of us like thrones.

II. SEVEN MINUTES IN HEAVEN
When Tommy H. spun the bottle, it landed on me, so I followed him into the closet, into dark so thick nothing changed when I blinked, which is what I'd always feared of death. Tommy banged his fist on the door in a lewd rhythm and moaned to muffled laughter from our friends, but he didn't try to touch me, didn't whisper, *Don't you want to*, didn't come close with his damp boy-breath, and I couldn't tell whether he was sparing me or teasing me, whether he was as unsure as I was or just thought me ugly.

III. MTV
At Stephanie's house after school, we'd watch *TRL*, Nelly Furtado's and Britney's bronzed midriffs writhing in dewy jungles or empty, white rooms. We'd talk about rumors—that Mr. Ableson had had a hard-on in class when Anna raised her hand, that Andrew B. had called Nina a Butterface at the mall, that Tara only ate white foods—until it was time for me to go.

Back home, in my room, I'd lift my shirt in front of the mirror and touch my ribs. Strum the bones of my cage splayed under my skin like umbrella spokes, like baby teeth ready to push through. I'd wonder who'd been lounging on some other couch that afternoon, talking about me.

IV. SELF-DEFENSE
After Ashley was assaulted behind the Burger King on Elmwood, our school arranged a self-defense class for the girls. We lined up in the gym like nervous birds on a wire. *Eyes, throat, groin!* the instructor yelled. As our shoes squeaked on shiny, yellow hardwood, I wanted to give up. In real life, my spindly limbs would never outmaneuver anyone. But, later, when we practiced our new moves in Anna's room, grabbing and wrestling, it was the most fun we'd had in a while. Heaving breaths, rug-burned, pink fingermarks blooming across our skin like petals.

V. 280 EMPIRE SERVICE
On the train to visit my older sister, I picked a window seat. I was tickling the edge of adulthood: a seven-hour

trip by myself, moving freely through the wide world alone. Every detail leapt, outsized. The navy nub of the Amtrak cushions, my backpack crowding my feet, the damp countryside trundling by. I imagined everyone on the train was secretly in love with me—*What an intriguing girl, there's something about her*—and I was in love with them, too. Later, after a college boy spoke to me in the dining car, wrote his email address on his ticket stub and slid it over the table, I caught my reflection in the window and, for a second, didn't recognize myself. I tried to see what everyone else saw, but by then it was my own face again, too familiar to judge. Smirking, uncertain, wary of the world but consumed by it.

The first sentence of "Girlhood Pentaptych" was previously published in slightly altered form as "Forest Lawn" in the fall 2022 issue of The Citron Review.

Frog

TIM RAYMOND

—

fiction

WHAT'S THE POOP? THE POOP IS MY SON FOUND a frog's leg in his kimchi at school, and now a journalist from Yonhap wants to interview him.

My son does not like attention, however, unless he's talking about something he loves, and that is not frogs. And thus, here is the conflict.

But, we talk awhile to the young woman at a Starbucks near Seohyun Station, and she seems very good at her job. And very good with kids in general, I suspect, if not with the atypical ones. The ones like my Hyojun.

She is throwing English words into her Korean sentences, perhaps on my account. And this is fine. It's fine.

Before going home, we pick up soondae since the place is right there and Wifey loves soondae. She will be so pleased, I think. We go home and Hera is pleased.

"Good job," she says to me.

I have a very nice marriage for which I am very grateful, despite what my intrusive thoughts say sometimes when it's hot and I can't sleep.

"Any problems?"

"With what?"

I realize she means the interview, so I say no. The school will take over now. The Ministry of Education will. Our part is done, and when the kimchi supplier is sued, we'll be unaffected.

"Hey, sweet child," says Hera.

She's a teacher of English and is great with our boy, in particular, if not with kids in general. She's currently a first-grade homeroom teacher at Bundang High School near Sunae Station.

Sometimes, I kid her about being an English teacher who's not fluent in English, which seems cruel except I only do it because it's our joke and she always gets the last laugh.

"And *you* are?" she'll say, which is funny because no, not with any sophistication I'm not. I am the reason Hyojun is atypical, I guess, and part of my atypicality is speech-related.

We met in Wyoming, my homeland, more than a decade ago. I was about to drop out of graduate school, and she, at 27 years old, had just passed the grueling teacher's examination. She was doing a bit of traveling before starting the job. Why she chose Wyoming instead of L.A. or Seattle like everybody else is beyond me. And to go *there* but not Yellowstone or Jackson Hole? She said she wanted to see the state's one university. A friend of a friend of a cousin, she said, spent a semester in Laramie. I met her at the Burger King and walked her to the Comfort Inn.

Evening passes, night passes. In the morning, I drive Hyojun to school then come home and start my work, which sometimes involves editing or proofreading for English teachers all around Seongnam. Mostly, it's writing fiction. The graduate program I dropped out of was for creative writing. Somehow, I emerged from this blunder, this fiasco of mine, and published a few short stories in decent magazines. And then, recently, I got an agent who's trying to sell my novel about autism and whales. The next one I'm writing is about a Shakespeare head, as I think of him, who vows revenge in a ranch town where I used to live. And there's an alien abduction too.

My agent is having some trouble, as far as I can tell.

Today is Wednesday, though, and that means there's a new episode of *Extraordinary Lawyer Woo*, which Hera loves and which I love, too, but also am hate-watching. After dinner, as Hyojun does his homework, we sit down and settle in. Ah, the latest case revolves around land compensation and a dispute between brothers.

This fucking show. Attorney Woo is all the autistic clichés all the time: echolalia, a verbal genius that allows her to memorize criminal law at five years old, a speech delay, an awkward gait, a photographic memory, some trouble reading facial expressions, flat affect and expression, diminished eye contact to the point of complete avoidance, a special interest related to animals, a routine she relies on, social deficits, an obsession with gimbap, which she eats every meal of every day.

Aversion to touch and sensitivity to sound! OCD tendencies, including threshold rituals! Her animals are whales, and about this I feel resentment!

I do love her, though. She is very beautiful and very cute and infantilized to the extent that it's very hard not to root for her for 70 minutes.

Sometimes, I wish my disability were more marketable. I am not cute, and people always think I'm angry. Maybe if I waddled like a penguin more, my stories would be adapted into #1 shows on Netflix. Their lead roles doled out to stars who are not disabled.

Or maybe I just need more pivotal poop scenes like in all the Korean programs. I poop all the time, a veritable shit*show*, so why not more plot devices related to diarrhea?

Instead, I look up interesting frog facts, like are any of them Shakespearean, I want to know, until it's me who's the frog boiling unawares. Oopsie, I am dehydrated and achy. I have ruined this writing session. Thursday now, and I am late picking up my son from school.

I am such a good driver. I am the wind. I leave our villa among the farm plots west of Yatap Station and zoom to Baekhyun Elementary.

"Do you want burgers?" I ask Hyojun. Yes, of course.

At the Flapjack Pantry, we order heaping plates. In addition to burgers and fries, we have pancakes with powdered sugar on them. I ask him how school was, but he only wants to discuss *Subnautica: Below Zero*, the ocean-world survivalist video game. I tried playing it, too, but got so overwhelmed and scared that I stopped. My boy is unphased by dark water and leviathan jaws.

He's found the habitat-builder tool, finally, after a week of searching for it, and now, instead of progressing the game's story, he is constructing an elaborate deep-water base among the Twisty Bridges.

"A sea monkey stole my flashlight," he says.

"Oh no."

At home, I'm on our one toilet because the burger set came with a free drink and *babo* me chose an Americano. Stupid, stupid. The poop seems endless.

"You're okay?" Hera knocks on the door and asks.

"No," I tell her.

But, because today is Thursday, there is another *Extraordinary Lawyer Woo* episode, and this is my reward for withstanding the intestinal distress. In this episode, we learn that autistics are incapable of lying.

Oh, damn, are they?

Here are the interesting frog facts I found before. Tell me which I'm making up: a frog sheds its skin every single week and usually eats what it sheds. When frogs swallow their prey, they blink, which presses their eyes down into their mouth, thereby directing the food matter into their throat. The frog's noun of assemblage is, of all things, army. Their brains are chock full of scorpions. Wait, that's Macbeth.

Hera has a stutter which I know she struggles with, but my idea that I want to believe in wholly is that someone talking infelicitously doesn't necessarily mean they're talking poorly. Everyone praises Attorney Woo when she speaks more typically in the courtroom. Meaning louder and more assertively. She was doing fine before, I like to tell Hera, who asks if we can please just enjoy the show.

The stutter shows up everywhere, yet it's least present when she's interacting with Hyojun, which I find so beautiful I ache a little.

I think a lot about this story I wrote 12 years ago in which a father takes his son around to different schools because he got kicked out of Poison Spider Elementary for always hanging out in the girls' bathroom. The son is essentially nonverbal, and the father is hardly articulate, so mostly they're wandering around confusing the administrative staffs. At the end of the day, they have visited five schools, and the son still has no place. At one point, the father accidentally enters the women's restroom.

How vehemently editors disliked this story! How offended they were that nothing happened in it! Excuse me, I am not bitter. I only think as an autistic person that everything is happening all the time. To be autie in the alli world is to live conflict ceaselessly. My every story boils down to this, I have realized.

Like now, God, this CGV movie theater, with its 4D horseshit. Hera likes Marvel movies, and anything related to special powers, and therefore we're watching the Thor sequel. Oh, Lord of Thunder, help us. Grant us reprieve from the lights and the noise and the people chewing popcorn right in front of us. Hyojun is asleep, it looks like. How.

In the lobby afterward, we eat hotdogs and pace around the arcade. I don't know what prompts me at first, but I start waddling around like a penguin. That bouncy, broad-footed slide that Attorney Woo uses. My boy, goodness, how he wordlessly mimics me. And it's not a joke for him or anything to call attention to; it's simply us being the masters of our own world.

You boy, you, don't you dare make me cry in the arcade, goddamn it. But, I do weep as he blasts zombies in *House of the Dead 4*.

It's almost exam season, so for two weeks I'm going to school every day to help various teachers make good English midterms. My labor is free for Hera because she's my wife and a goddess and has changed my life irrevocably for the better and snores a lot most nights and on Sundays if I interrupt her making her milk tea and listening to KBO news on YouTube she gets annoyed.

At Bulgok High School, and who's to say what prompts me this time, I start talking like Attorney Woo. Attorney Woo when she's in her dad's gimbap restaurant and droning on. Attorney Woo arranging ham slices into an X because the new ham supplier is bogus.

"Are you okay?" the teachers say.

"I didn't sleep very well last night," I tell them, though it's not true.

The next night, it's true. Oh, villainy, these rotten scorpions who visit their venom upon me: you don't make nearly enough money, you layabout fuck. What man makes his wife bring home the bacon? You sit in that room all day, typing nonsense that nobody reads. You could have gone back to school to become a pharmacy technician, but instead you got married, you codependent cur. You lily-livered narcissist. You relief-seeking hermit. You had a kid because you're selfish, you're weak, you're afraid your voice wouldn't have otherwise lived on, and for immense shame. The world's dying.

One thing about healing for me is seeing not only that your thoughts aren't yours but that they're boring and uninspired. Would I read that conflict there to its very end? Likely not.

I have, nevertheless, come to in the parking lot outside. The many cats from the hanok-style home across the street crawl from beneath silver cars to drag their matted butts against my shins.

What's the poop? There's some soil in my underwear now. Crohn's, maybe? Classic IBS! I do wonder about this grease! The happening poop is my occasional psychosis.

At another high school, I walk down the hallway with my hands over my ears because the cool kids with their slick watches are shouting at each other about what's for lunch. They're so blinded by their own ease that they back up into a mousy girl with thinning hair who's just trying to pass the day without incident. Then, they ask me for a high-five, which I ignore.

I used to worry that Hyojun would get bullied, but it just doesn't seem to happen to him. His gaming prowess means the other boys envy him. Plus, he's tall. Life can be hard for multicultural kids, but his dad is American and white, so that helps. Plus, he's handsome, even though I'm not so much.

When I was in high school, some older kids asked me to come hang out at the lake with them then proceeded to throw both me and my car keys into the water. I did get home the next day, if a bit worse for wear. Rest assured that nobody will be throwing our son into any lakes or ponds or seas. No oceans or reservoirs or sounds or tributaries. Certainly not the Han River.

At the same time, I do know of parents who have scolded Hera for suggesting their kids were maybe ADHD or autistic. How vehemently they despised these comments! How scandalized they were by them! How quick to phone the vice principal!

"They're struggling," she'll try to explain.

"So, encourage them more!"

Which, this is just to say, I'm thankful for what I have.

At the third high school, there's a question on the exam about frogs. It's one of those that asks which underlined sentences have a grammatical

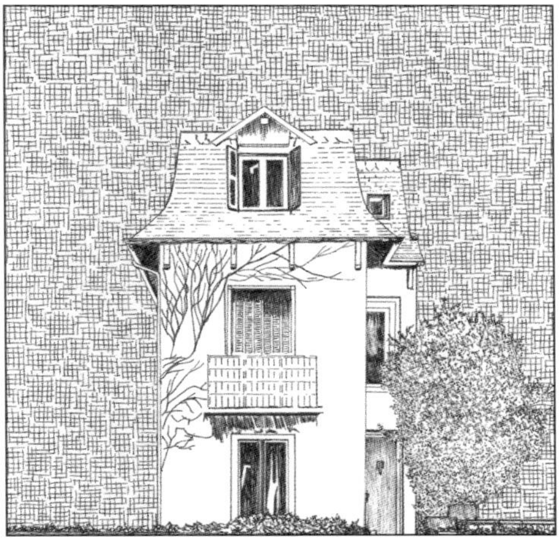

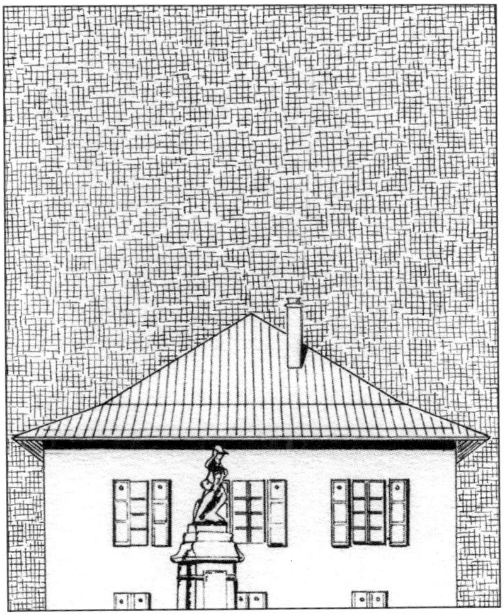

error in them. Sometimes, I can't access the things I know. Sometimes, all I want is for ideas to be exchanged so that we can move forward already.

The frogs does this so that . . . while live in the tree, they . . . the frog in Indonesia lives a whole life without lungs, as it breathes entirely via the skin . . . which it shed daily . . .

I breathing person seeing hornet in room we're being in.

"Uh oh," I say aloud.

It doesn't sting me, but the teacher I'm with flails suddenly, and this upsets the hornet, who zeroes in on her. After the attack, it bolts straight to the open window as though it knew all along where its path to freedom lay.

At home that night, I try to tell the story to my family yet get confused when I'm reminded I speak only Korean to Hera and only English to Hyojun. Triangulated in this manner, I start mixing and matching, and there is no method to my madness, and the garbled and disorganized mess of ideas is not properly exchanged.

"What?" asks Hera.

Hornets are generally shy, the internet tells me later, and only become aggressive if they believe their territory is being significantly threatened.

Only the females, I read on, possess stingers.

They also hibernate and during this period subsist on stores of nectar.

That weekend we travel to Pyeongtaek to have a playdate with our friends Sunny and Darren, who are rich and multicultural and whose daughter is around Hyojun's age. After relating the story of the attack in English, I share with them the three hornet facts that I remember, to which they say they know nothing about the insects and have never seen one in real life even.

The kids are staring at one another. Their daughter is an extrovert through and through, and meanwhile our son is a closed cupboard full of the most nutritious and delicious food items available on the market.

He keeps blinking. To swallow, I muse, this activity he wants no part of.

The park we're at has twisty trees like the Twisty Bridges, though, and as with everything in life things are vastly improved once we start walking. The mommies talk TV and the frog's leg. Darren tells me how his work's been going. America denied him a visa recently, but he still gets to keep his job coding for an investment firm in Manhattan. If he had his way and could swing it, he'd rather be designing crossword puzzles or writing some kind of interactive, visual-novel type of game in which kids can learn about themselves and others.

"And the whale pandemic?" he says to me.

"The *what*?"

Ah, he means my novel. Billions of humans have been transformed into beluga whales to either perish on dry land or compete for resources in whichever body of water is closest. The meek who inherit the earth are the divergents, whose neurology acts like an immunizing agent. It's wild.

"I don't know," I tell him and open my email. "Let me check. Hang on."

"Yep."

"No news," I report then, which is true only for another hour or so. By this point, we have climbed up a small mountain near the park and gotten lost on its convoluted system of trails. Because reasons, the paths are not clearly delineated, unlike in Seoul. Darren dislikes hiking, actually, and so has begun to despair. His daughter is chasing butterflies that lure her into uneven, perilous terrain. Hyojun is sitting in the middle of the trail, while Hera and Sunny ask for advice from strangers who are also lost. It's then that I move to pull up Naver Maps and instead out of habit click on Gmail.

"Well, they said they liked it," my agent explains. "So, there's that. But, it just didn't feel right for them. Onward and to the next one, man. Forget about it, okay?"

Okay, but excuse me for a sec while I tattoo these lines on my chest and sleep shirtless and on my back for the rest of eternity. Angels, glimpse me. The placeless poet. No, I'm kidding. I used to be broken by rejection but now am too tired to be. Plus, I have a family who thinks I'm right for them even when they don't like me. Like now, when I'm useless trash with helping to navigate.

Yet, we do eventually get off the mountain. And it's Hyojun who's the one to lead us out. It's probable he knew the way the entire time. Boy, that pokerface and nose for exploration. Anyway, we're all sweaty and over it, and I won't say who, but somebody here had to make the trees their toilet.

The rejection breaks me every time, in fact, and this makes what I said before a heinous lie. Now, I see the break coming as I descend the stairs into Yatap Station on my way to Nupeulin High School for more exams. I pass the advertisement for the urologist who checked my penis that time the health anxiety commandeered me and I mistook dehydration for something fatal. There's the dentist who wrenched my wisdom teeth from my dizzy skull. On the train, I plug into a dramatization of *Hamlet* for research and for comfort because tell me about the quintessence of dust, you prince. I can't hear the monologue because these 20-somethings in the middle of the car are shouting.

Uh oh. Meltdown. Easy there, big guy. It's not an assault on you that they like soccer, even if your sensitive earsies say otherwise. But, no, clashing voices can really get to me.

When it's over, I've yelled some and paced some and knocked into some people who are only trying to be alive and then apologized to them to the best of my ability. Oh, heavy deed! I tell them that I'm genuinely the shy hornet. If I react like this, fellow subway passengers, it's only because some part of my territory feels threatened. Passengers of the yellow Shin-Bundang Line, I have no stinger, see, for I am but a man!

I tell them I hibernated a whole lot of my life, just years gone, because I never knew how to participate in a way that didn't systematically erode me. And while hibernating, I did binge on various harmful nectars. So, please believe that I'm trying my best.

None of it, I'm fully aware, will translate all that well. I think at one point I said I fell into the addiction of honey.

At home that evening, I tell Hera she's my honey wasp. My queen. My Ophelia, worth 40,000 lovers. I say, "O, ye gods! Render me worthy of this noble Wifey!"

"Stop it," she stammers.

"Okay."

I'm interrupting *Extraordinary Lawyer Woo*, and in our house that's a sin. In this one, a North Korean defector accused of robbery and assault and who was on the lamb for years is desperately trying to get a mitigated sentence so that she doesn't have to spend too much time away from her daughter, who's either sleeping or sobbing the entire episode. By the end of it, I'm not sure who I'm crying for. Is it Attorney Woo, whose mother abandoned her for some mysterious reason? Is it the refugee, our world's truly placeless, who gets probation and thanks everyone in the courtroom for understanding her plight? Or is it I, who never sees my own mother, my own mother who was supplanted by my *eomeonim*, who's always trying to put some pickled vegetable or other into my mouth?

Ah, no, it's the music. A soaring soundtrack will get me every time. Shows, movies, commercials, even radio jingles.

"How do you say melodrama in Korean?" I ask Hera, who sniffs.

The next day, we go to Jamsil for the baseball game, because apparently Wifey wants to see Doosan kick the shit out of Hanhwa, her team. That's fair enough. We go and buy hot dogs at the stand, and I eat three of them until I'm slowed way, way down. When inevitably I go to the bathroom, Hyojun comes with me and not to pee or anything but just to hang out together. We waddle through the arteries of the stadium and buy plastic cups of ice that we suck on. Outside, I think, Hera snaps photos while the Bears fans chant their chants.

In our seats again, the kid fires up *Subnautica: Below Zero* on his Switch and mutters to himself about some hidden alien artifact he still can't find. I pop in my earplugs, bought special from the UK, to mute the damn everything. But, it means I can't hear Hera in any detail as she talks about someone she used to know who lives around here. I count how many times the pitcher requests a clean ball from the umpire.

Have some perspective, Attorney Woo, would you? Seven. She tells her dad that on account of her autism, she'll likely never be able to marry. Eight. Just chill out, okay? Nine. Have some gimbap and relax a bit. Ten. A foul ball is hit beyond the first-base line, in our direction, and I catch it barehanded before it wallops my only child. I give the ball to him, and he gives it to the woman next to him, who gives it to her husband, who gives it to a grandfatherly type figure, who gives it to a child, whose joy is unequivocal. You're smart, Attorney Woo. You can see this line of benevolence and love on which we all reside. We, all of us, the aliens included.

On the train home, I save myself the trouble and read a short story online instead of finishing the *Hamlet* performance on Scribd. Boy, and it's a doozy: yet another in a trend of stories using sad, dead, or suicidal autistic kids as plot tricks in service of some typical adult's emotional arc.

This secondary character has destroyed a marriage, at which point my heart wants to rage. Thrust my rapier into your threadbare tapestry, story! But, I scabbard that motherfucker, for methinks the person doth protest too much. And it's fine, really. It is. Carry on, Poloniuses, to thine own selves be true.

Because as I stand shoulder to shoulder in a hot subway box, as I climb the stairs at Yatap Station shoulder to shoulder with strangers and smokers and talkers, as I stand in line for soondae at a busy shop in a busy market with cooks screaming and bustling and clanging dishes together so loud it hurts me and I go mute while ordering: as I gesture to Hyojun that Dad needs a moment, all right, and look upon his face as it contorts into tantrum and bow slightly to Hera that she might take over for me, please and thank you, and finally while walking home by the Tancheon my language jumbles and I forget the word for white, skyward fluff then momentarily am blind to the bigness of all creatures and beings, I *know* my babo brain is lying to me when it says I should jump ship and drown. In any case, the water in that stream is far too shallow. This life's brilliant, man, and if you want proof, go check the koi fish gathered like family by the footbridge.

While We Can

DAN REITER

—

fiction

WHEN ABIGAIL STRETCHED OUT HER ARMS AND chirped in her sweet, piping voice, "We're *all* going to die!" we couldn't help but laugh because Abigail was a nine-year-old child and, in the afternoon glow of the playground, with the sparrows playing accompaniment, her words sounded so implausible, so absurd, as if they weren't true at all.

In February, our parents grew gills in front of their ears and went to coughing and hiccupping. It was the same year we put the dog down—poor thing. She took the injection and melted into my lap, limp and lifeless as a mink stole. But her eyes were still open, still glistening at me with that old trust. I closed them with my fingertips, like I'd seen in the movies. A sob escaped my throat, involuntary as laughter.

At the onset of the thing, when everyone stopped kissing and embracing and the boomers began to grapple their chests and spar for air, we wondered if maybe it wasn't their karmic reward. Burying the earth in trash heaps, shearing off all the old growth, murking the waters in the rime of chemicals and plastics. Such a careless reign. Consumers, boomers, tumors. White, insatiable, swollen, growing more spiteful by the season.

But when the lights among them—those who'd shown bravery and finesse—began to flicker out, we repented our evil thoughts, and our anger dissolved like sugar into coffee.

The schools closed, and we stocked up on canned beans and fever-reducers and slow-cooked chicken soup until the house was redolent with onions and schmaltz, like my Bubbe's old apartment in Hallandale Beach. I read Tolkien aloud to the children, and they ate everything and thickened with muscle and seemed impervious. My wife and I made love every night, and we fell asleep watching song-and-dance numbers from the 1950s. Summer came, and nothing changed. The sun hung out back like a ripe gold peach.

The word *pandemic*, we learned, is derived from the Greek word *pan*, which meant "all," and *demos*, for "people."

I promised the children I'd look for a new dog, and in June I drove a couple of hours out of town and came home with a brindle puppy that could pass for the brood of our recently departed, only with a corkscrew tail and confused, bulbous eyes. We huddled on the couch and caressed the creature and scrolled through luminous images of our past selves. The children giggled at their baby-faced miniatures, which seemed to them surreal approximations of reality.

Two years prior, on the stony grasslands of Crowheart, Wyoming, our heads tilted to the sky, we stared through eclipse binoculars at the fiery nimbus encircling the sun. Our bodies stood slack, in shock or submission, as if our mother star had been extinguished and here was her remnant smoke. We watched the corona uncoil in wisps of irradiant energy, and then the sun flared out from its hiding place, the darkness rushed east, and the hills awakened from the false night.

Now, in a conclave of a different sort, we wait as the corona dances and unravels around us. The distance between our present and past selves expands like an impassable sea. We had been reluctant, then, to accept the idea that the sun and the moon could be exactly the same size. It seemed a ruse, an unthinkable coincidence.

But we learn to ask such questions. To live while we can. And after a few glasses of wine, we can still bring ourselves to laugh at the thing Abigail had said. So naive, so sensible, in the end.

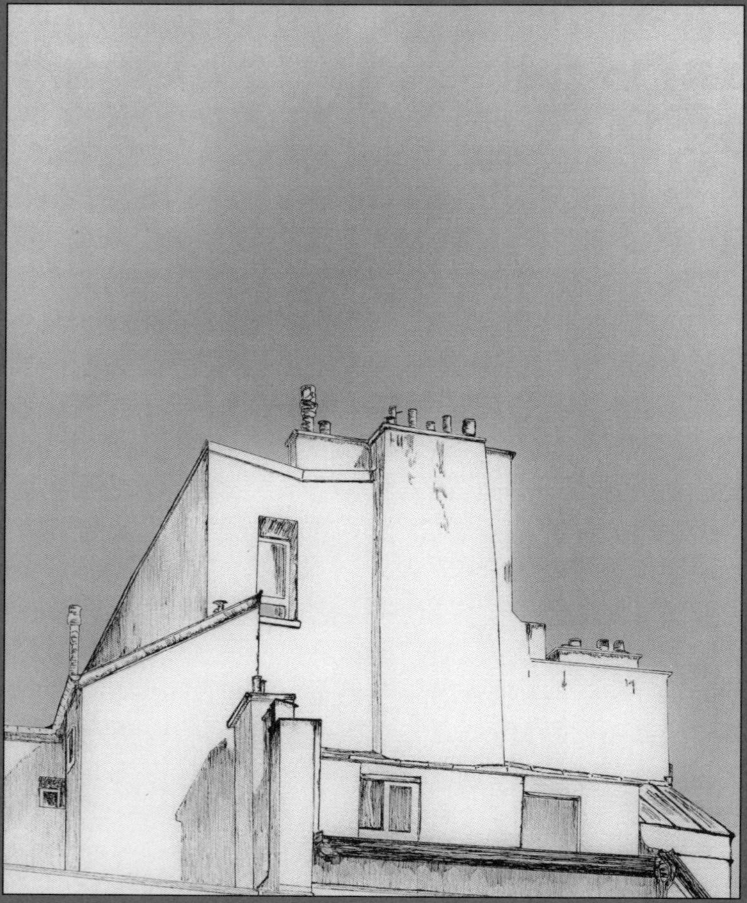

About the Artist
Michael Dahlie

Michael Dahlie received an NEA Fellowship in 2020 for his illustrated fiction. The images here are illustrations from long-form fiction projects, heroically transposed by the editors at *Booth*.

Dahlie is the author of two novels (without pictures), and his fiction has appeared in places like *Harper's*, *The Yale Review*, and *Electric Literature*. He's received the PEN/Hemingway Award, a Pushcart Prize, and a Whiting Award, and he's currently Associate Professor in Butler University's English Department and MFA Program. More of his work can be found on his Instagram feed @michaeldahlie.

Contributors

Jerilynn Aquino is a Puerto Rican writer from New Jersey. Her essays and poetry appear in *Salt Hill*, *The Journal*, *Gulf Coast*, *Reed Magazine*, and others. She is the recipient of a 2023 Hedgebrook Writing Residency and a 2022 AWP Intro Journals Award in Nonfiction. She is currently pursuing her Ph.D. in Creative Writing at Oklahoma State University. You can find her online at www.jerilynnaquino.com.

nicole v basta's recent poems have found homes in *Ploughshares*, *Waxwing*, *Plume*, *RHINO*, *North American Review*, *The Cortland Review*, and *Best New Poets 2023*. She is the author of the chapbook *the next field over* (2022) from Tolsun Books and V (2017), the winner of The New School's Annual Contest. nicole is also a visual artist, community educator, and arts events curator with proud roots in the Pennsylvania coal mines & garment factories.

Michael Beard (he/him) holds an MFA in Poetry from Bowling Green State University. His poems have appeared or are forthcoming in *Variant Literature*, *Pine Hills Review*, *Moon City Review*, and other places. He currently lives in Tennessee and teaches Dual Enrollment English at local high schools.

Mialise Carney is a writer and editor whose stories have appeared in *swamp pink*, *Barren Magazine*, and *The Boiler*, among others. She reads fiction for *Alien Magazine* and poetry for *Best of the Net*. Read more of her work at mialisecarney.com.

Willow James Claire (James O'Leary) is a trans poet from Arizona. Their work has been nominated for Best of the Net and a Pushcart Prize and has appeared in such journals as *Frontier*, *Protean*, *The Indianapolis Review*, and *Foglifter*. Willow holds an MFA from Sarah Lawrence College and currently serves as a poetry reader for both *Little Patuxent Review* and *ANMLY*.

Hannah Cohen is the author of two poetry chapbooks from Glass Poetry Press: *Year of the Scapegoat* (2022) and *Bad Anatomy* (2018). Hannah co-edits the online literary journal *Cotton Xenomorph*. Recent and forthcoming publications include *Poetry Currency*, *Michigan Quarterly Review*, *Hey Alma*, *Pidgeonholes*, *The Offing*, and others. She was a 2018 Best of the Net finalist and a Pushcart Prize nominee.

Courtney Craggett is the author of the story collection *Tornado Season* (Black Lawrence Press, 2019). Her short stories appear in *The Pinch*, *Mid-American Review*, *Baltimore Review*, *Washington Square Review*, *CutBank*, and *Monkeybicycle*, among others. She holds a Ph.D. in creative writing from the University of North Texas and teaches at Weber State University.

Jennifer Delgadillo is a Mexican American artist and writer living in the Near Eastside of Indianapolis. She is a student in the Butler University MFA program and the arts and culture editor at mirrorindy.org.

K.S. Dyal is the author of the novella *It Felt Like Everything* (Ad Hoc Fiction, 2022). Her work appears in the *Colorado Review*, *Carve*, *Quarterly West*, *HAD*, *Pithead Chapel*, and elsewhere. She writes from Washington, D.C.

Sam Fouts grew up in the Cleveland area and is currently studying creative writing at Miami University. His work has been nominated for a Pushcart Prize and appears in *Sky Island Journal*, *The Drable*, *Flash Fiction Magazine*, and elsewhere.

Fee Griffin is a writer and poet from England. Her second collection, *Really Not Really*, was published with Broken Sleep Books (2023) and is available in the US through Barnes and Noble. Her debut poetry collection, *For Work/For TV* was published in 2020 with Versal Editions and won the Amsterdam Open Book Prize. She was a founding poetry editor at *The Lincoln Review* and has recent work published in *Granta*, *Poetry London*, *The Rialto*, *Magma*, *Stand*, and *Peach Mag*, among others. She works part time as an Associate Lecturer at the University of Lincoln and has the fastest orange wheelchair you've ever seen.

Jesse Lee Kercheval is a writer, translator, and visual artist. Her most recent books include the story collection *Underground Women* and the poetry collections *I Want to Tell You* and *America that island off the coast of France*, winner of the Dorset Prize.

Rachel Salguero Kowalsky is a Guatemalan American writer, pediatric emergency physician, three-time Pushcart Prize nominee, and winner of the *NEJM* short-fiction contest. Her stories appear in *The Missouri Review*, *Atticus Review*, *Orca*, *jmww*, *Intima: A Journal of Narrative Medicine*, and elsewhere. She is grateful to Maynor Ajcalón Hernandez, Celestino Sajvin Sajvin, Joyce Bennett, and Lauren McNaughton for their careful review and Ixnal Cuma de Chanquín who reflected: At the heart of every story es un ser humano.

Naomi Bess Leimsider's poetry book, *Wild Evolution*, was published by Cathexis Northwest Press in June 2023. In addition, she has published poems, flash fiction, and short stories in numerous journals, including *Unleash Lit*, *Packingtown Review*, *Tangled Locks Journal*, *The Avenue Journal*, *Anti-Heroin Chic*, *Wild Roof Journal*, *Syncopation Literary Journal*, *On the Seawall*, *St. Katherine Review*, *Exquisite Pandemic*, *Orca*, *Hamilton Stone Review*, *Rogue Agent Journal*, *Otis Nebula*, *Quarterly West*, and *The Adirondack Review*. She has been a finalist for the Acacia Fiction Prize and the Saguaro Poetry Prize. In 2022, she received a Pushcart Prize nomination for fiction.

Susan Lerner received her MFA in Creative Writing from Butler University. She serves as assistant memoir editor for *Split Lip Magazine*, assistant editor for *Brevity*, and reads for *River Teeth*, *TriQuarterly*, and *Fourth Genre*. Her work has appeared in *The Rumpus*, *The Believer Logger*, *Painted Bride Quarterly*, and elsewhere. Find her on Instagram @susanlitelerner and online at Susan-Lerner.com.

Hannah Marshall lives in Grand Rapids, Michigan, where she works at the public library. Her poetry has been published in *The Best American Poetry*, *New Ohio Review*, *The American Journal of Poetry*, and elsewhere. Her manuscript, *The Shape That Good Can Take*, was a finalist for the 2021 St. Lawrence Book Award. She received her MFA in Creative Writing from Converse University.

Calgary Martin is originally from Washington State but spent her formative years in Brooklyn, NY. Her poems appear in *Hayden's Ferry Review, Cimarron Review, The Gettysburg Review,* and *Tupelo Quarterly,* among others. She lives in Illinois with her husband and their two kids.

Justin Noga is a writer out of Akron, Ohio. His work can be found/is forthcoming in *Conjunctions, Bennington Review, The Arkansas International, Columbia Journal, Reed Magazine, Witness,* and *Northwest Review.* He lives in Arizona. Find him on Instagram @jus.tin.no.ga, and justinnoga.com.

Adrián Pérez is a writer and designer living in Brooklyn, NY. He holds an MFA in Fiction from Columbia University, where he served as Editor-in-Chief of *Columbia Journal.* He is currently finishing work on his first novel, a multi-character narrative about losing and gaining power during a global catastrophe. When not writing, he enjoys traveling, figuring out what his cats are thinking, and perfecting his grandmother's salsa recipe.

Erin Pinkham is a queer poet from North Texas. Her work focuses on coming-of-age, girlhood, and queer issues inspired by life in the South on her family's tomato farm. They are currently a poetry MFA candidate at the University of Arkansas. In addition to the topic of poetics, she will often be heard gushing about anime, spellcasting, her dog Willie, pink-velvet fabric, and the Korean boyband BTS.

Tim Raymond works as a barista in South Korea. His fiction has appeared recently or will appear in *Boulevard, CRAFT,* and *Conjunctions,* among others. Find his comics on Instagram at @iamsitting.

Dan Reiter's experiments with the short form have appeared in *Bellevue Literary Review, American Short Fiction, Kenyon Review, Tin House,* and elsewhere. Recent work is forthcoming in *The New Yorker, Harper's Magazine,* and *The Paris Review* slush piles.

Claire Stanford is the author of the novel *Happy for You,* which was named a *New York Times* Book Review Editors' Choice and awarded the 2023 Janet Heidinger Kafka Prize for Fiction, among other honors. Her writing has appeared in *Black Warrior Review, The Rumpus, Tin House Flash Fridays, Electric Lit, Lit Hub,* the *Los Angeles Review of Books,* and elsewhere. Born and raised in

Berkeley, she currently lives in Reno, where she is an assistant professor at the University of Nevada, Reno.

Maggie Yang is a writer and artist from Vancouver, Canada. Recognized by The Poetry Society and *The Adroit Journal*, her work has been published in *The Florida Review, Split Rock Review,* and *Gulf Stream Magazine,* among others.

Mimi Yang's work appears or is forthcoming in *The Penn Review, Palette Poetry,* and *The Greensboro Review,* among others. They are a Best of the Net Nominee and a Foyle Commended Young Poet, and they currently attend Brown University. They are always dreaming of liberation.

Booth thanks the following for their generous support:

Jay Anderson

Lisa Bass

Kara Duff Bungard

Adam Crozier

Nathan Holic

Samantha Karels

Jennifer Serafyn